101 Ways
— *to* —
Nourish Your Soul

101 Ways
— to —
Nourish Your Soul

MITCH FINLEY

A Crossroad Book
The Crossroad Publishing Company
New York

1996

The Crossroad Publishing Company
370 Lexington Avenue, New York, NY 10017

Copyright © 1996 by Mitch Finley

Printed in the United States of America

Library of Congress Cataloging-in-Publication Data

Finley, Mitch.
    101 ways to nourish your soul / Mitch Finley.
      p. cm.
    ISBN 0-8245-1589-7 (pbk.)
    1. Spiritual life. I. Title.
  BL624.F517   1996
  158—dc20   96-20590
                              CIP

This book is for
James Lee and Pearl Burke

Little my soul,
You and I are the same...

—Mark Van Doren,
"Little My Soul"

Contents

Acknowledgments

Many thanks to friends who helped me to think of ways to nourish one's soul, in particular Antoinette Bosco and Bob Cubbage. Special thanks to Rene Kehrwald for her insights and wisdom on the art and benefits of massage therapy. Thanks to my spouse and constant inspiration, Kathy Finley, for support and encouragement. These people generously offered suggestions, but the final form and commentaries are my own. Therefore, any inanities in the text are my responsibility alone.

Soul and Body:
The Best of Friends

"Soul" is a word with a checkered past. Earlier generations thought of the human soul as a kind of invisible self, a ghost even, the real you that would survive after you expire. Many assumed that body and soul were opposed to each other, the body an ongoing threat to the soul and its ultimate destiny. Decades ago some sage delivered himself of the opinion that the soul was actually located in a particular part of the human anatomy, near the base of the skull, invisible and about the size of a grape.

A more contemporary view suggests that soul and body are not two different parts of the human person, as if the soul had simply taken up temporary residence, riding around in the body for the duration. Rather, human beings are best described as *embodied spirits*. Whatever is bodily is also spiritual, and whatever is spiritual is also bodily.

The old view had this much going for it. When we die our soul survives — or is transformed by — the death process. The soul is the spiritual principle of the human being that goes on living after death — whatever a "spiritual principle" may be. This does not mean, however, that your soul and your body are only incidentally or accidentally related to each other. Rather, they are the most intimate of friends and companions. Each has the other's better welfare at heart, because what's good for the one is good for the other.

Even more than that, body and soul support and depend upon each other. When you hug someone you love, that is your soul expressing love as much as your body. You can't express your soul's love for another unless your body expresses that love too. When you worship, meditate, or pray, your body is involved in these actions as much as your soul. Your soul can't pray, worship, or meditate unless your brain and the rest of your body pray too. You can't send your soul off to pray while your body remains in bed or goes someplace else to get some work done. We're talking intimate teamwork here.

All the suggestions in this book about nourishing your soul are, therefore, suggestions for nourishing your whole self in the light of your spirituality. The focus is on the soul because it is so easy to overlook our spiritual dimension in everyday matters. It is also true, of course, that it is easy to overlook our bodiliness, or revert unconsciously to the old mistake of despising our body, when we focus on our spirituality. The former is a bigger risk than the latter, however.

The key to the cultivation of a balanced, healthy spirituality is to keep in mind that anything we believe about our physical being we must believe about our spiritual being. Our spirituality must be feminine or masculine, for example, because we cannot act apart from our gender. Our spirituality is emotional because we are emotional beings. It is impossible to overemphasize the intimacy or unity between soul and body.

At the same time, we can't say that soul and body are absolutely identified with each other. A mentally and/or physically handicapped person is just as human as a so-called "normal" person. Often, in fact, in some ways a person with Down's syndrome, for example, manifests a deeper spirituality than that of the average "normal" person. He or she reveals a capacity for love that often exceeds that of "normal" people. Sometimes normality leads us to make selfish choices that frustrate the soul's longing to love and be loved. That's one reason it's important to practice explicitly "spiritual" ways to nourish ourselves, to strive for human balance. That's one reason it's important to nourish your soul.

Please accept the 101 ways to nourish your soul that this book offers in the spirit in which they were written: a spirit of dialogue, creativity, and good humor. Take each suggestion as a starting point for your own unique reflections and soul-nourishing actions. Be open to the special manifestations of the Divine Mystery in your own life. Above all, be kind to yourself, and be kind to those with whom you share the earth; be kind to the earth itself, and know that you were created for joy....

1 ◆ *Listen to Your Soul*

WE LISTEN to so much, and we listen to so little. Listen. Let it be. Just listen. Take a minute, a mere minute each day, and listen to your deepest center. Listen to what your soul may tell you. Listen. The soul speaks what we most need to hear, if we listen. So listen.

At the core of your being there is silence. "The still center of the turning world," poet T. S. Eliot called it. We send space shuttles into orbit in outer space to drift among the stars. We throw out a highly sophisticated telescope to spin through space and focus even farther into the unknown, sending its images back to earth for scientists to marvel at and puzzle over. Amazing. But the universe has another center, one much closer to home.

The universe has a center in each one of us, and we can listen to it. When you listen to your soul you listen to your own union with the Divine Mystery at the heart of the universe. You do. Amazing. Smack your forehead with an open hand and sit down, whump, it is so astonishing. There is no greater mystery than this one. There is not.

Listen to your own soul, to your own amazing union with the Divine Mystery at the heart of the universe, and know that this same Mystery dwells at the deepest center of every human being. Each and every human being on the earth. Even you. Know this and smack your forehead with an open hand in amazement. Think about it long enough, ponder the fact at length, and you may have a tough time not falling down to worship the next person you see. It's possible. It is.

Sit still. Close your eyes. Don't think about anything. Get a blank mind, then focus on your own inner being. Listen. The still center of the turning world. The Divine Mystery at the heart of the universe lives in you. Listen. Here is your beginning, and here is your end. Here is your path all along the way. Believe it.

"The unexamined life is not worth living." It was true centuries ago when Aristotle first said it, and it's true today. It will always be true. Those who live with some depth live consciously, live with awareness, do not go through life sleep-walking, spiritually speaking. They try to live thoughtfully, honestly, and with purpose. It's not difficult, although many people make it so. All you need do is listen to your own soul and you will learn the truth. Listen.

This is the foundation, the essential basis for a life worth living. Listen to the Divine Mystery in your soul and you shall live.

2 ◆ *Begin Your Day with Prayer*

MORNING. A new day. You open your eyes after hours of sleep and dreams. You open your eyes and do not give it a second thought, do you not? You wake to another day. No big deal. Ho hum. But look. You woke up. You are still alive. You have another day in a string of days that, one day, will come to a screeching halt. You get only so many hours, minutes, and seconds, and no more. Finitude, it's called. Mortality, it's called.

This is a wonder, this waking up every day to a new day. It's a wonder that we don't see the wonder of it all. Your soul knows, but because new days happen over and over and over and over and . . . Your soul knows the wonder of each new day, but how often do you listen to your soul? You take it for granted. Everyone does. But it's good for us, down deep, if we give ourselves a shake now and then and remember the wonder of it all. The wonderful joy of having another day to live. Countless people who had yesterday to live don't have today because yesterday, or last night, they bought the farm. They do not have today. But you do. It boggles the mind.

See here. We're not talking about a Pollyanna outlook on life and the world. Maybe you woke up this morning and remembered that you are unemployed. Major bummer. Or maybe you woke up with a terrible cold, or the flu, or a vaginal yeast infection, or a testicular infection. Oo. Perhaps you opened your eyes this morning only to know, again, that you have a terminal illness. Perhaps you are old and tired and sick. Every new day isn't a day on Sunnybrook Farm.

That's reality, whatever you woke up to this morning. That's reality, and that's the stuff prayer is made of. So begin your day with prayer. Lie in your bed, or stand at the window, or kneel down. Speak silently to the Divine Mystery in your own deepest center. Speak silently to the Divine Mystery present in love at the heart of the universe and in its farthest reaches.

Say whatever comes into your noggin, or say a prayer you know by heart. "Our Father..." "Hear, O Israel..." "Om manipadmi om..." "Hail, Mary..." "Bless the Lord, O my soul..." "All praise is due to Allah, the Lord of the Worlds."

Clam up and give your soul a chance to speak honestly to the Divine Mystery at its own deepest center. If it's an ordinary day, your prayer may be routine. If it's a day of unemployment or sickness, your prayer may be a prayer of complaint and begging for help or a prayer of anger. All that matters is prayer at the start of a new day. No matter how you feel, each new day is a gift...and there is no telling, no telling at all, what this day will bring. Open your soul to the new day. Open your soul through prayer.

3 ◆ *End Your Day with Prayer*

TYPICALLY, how do you end your day? Do you groan yourself out of an overstuffed chair, or off a couch, after hours of staring at a television screen? Do you drag yourself home at 9:00

or 10:00 p.m. after long, long hours at a job that does not nourish your soul but pays the bills? Or that does nourish your soul and pay the bills? Do you stumble into bed after the daily hassle of getting the kids off to bed? Or what?

Regardless of how your day ends, do you end your day or does your day end you? You can end your day if you bring it to a close with prayer. No matter what kind of work you do, no matter how you spend your time during the day, and no matter how you spend the last few hours before you crawl between the sheets, you can nourish your soul by ending your day with prayer. You can. If you choose to you can.

This day, this day that is over now, has been a day filled with the ordinary. What did you do? Days are filled with the consequences of the choices we made, the consequences of choices others made for us, and the consequences of sheer happenstance. All these things give us the day we had today. There it is...or, rather, there it was. It's over now.

Here's a wild idea. Before you sink into sleep, pause for a moment and ask yourself about the day you just had. How do you feel about it? Be aware of how you feel about it. Right down to your toes, how do you feel about the day you had? Now. While you brush your teeth, or while you get into your nightgown or pajamas — or, wonderful sensuous you, as you undress to sleep in the nude — say a prayer. Yes.

The toothpaste is foaming in your mouth as you scrub away at your molars and incisors. Pray whatever is in your heart. Pulling off your shoes and socks, pray. Unhooking your bra and peeling off your pantyhose, pray. My feet are killing me. My eyes are tired. My back is sore. It's been a good day, a satisfying day, but I'm tired. This is the kind of day it has been — God, Creator, Allah, Jesus, Whoever — and this is how I feel about it. Just touching bases, just turning my heart to You. Just coming home, bringing my soul and body to You. God, Creator, Allah, Jesus, Whoever. Love at the heart of the universe.

Some find it easier to use a rote prayer, a memorized prayer, a prayer that comes trippingly to the tongue, that requires not so much thought, something with some poetry to it, some built-in structure and beauty. Some do. "Let my evening prayer ascend before you, O Lord. And let your loving kindness descend upon us." Some people like to use a prayer book, a collection of prayers to read from. You could do worse at the end of the day when you're tired.

4 ◆ *Do Work You Enjoy*

PEOPLE of a certain age remember an early 1960s television sitcom. The two main characters were Dobie Gillis and his pal Maynard G. Krebbs. Maynard was a good-hearted young 1950s beatnik wannabe (although the term "wannabe" didn't exist yet). If anyone ever mentioned work, he would exclaim, "Work!" in a funny tone of voice that said, "This is something I really can't cope with; anything but work."

You see those bumper stickers and license plate frames that announce that the driver would rather be doing something else. "I'd rather be skiing," "I'd rather be flying," or "I'd rather be shopping." The driver of the car would rather be doing something other that what he or she is doing. The ordinary, everyday world is a drag. Work, especially, is a drag. Blecch.

So you may ask, "How can work nourish my soul?" One may reply that if the work you do does not nourish your soul then you should find another line of work. Easy to say, not so easy to do. The title of a best-selling book, *Do What You Love, the Money Will Follow,* is a misleading oversimplification of mountainous proportions.

Modern societies often make it difficult for people to do work that nourishes the soul. Does working in a fast food hamburger restaurant nourish the soul? Does working in a "fast-lube" garage nourish the soul? Does fitting the same microchip into a printed circuit board over and over all day long nourish the soul? It's perfectly possible that some people like such forms of work and find it a soul-nourishing experience. Some few people, at least. Many would not find fast food work nourishing, however. Many. And many would not find giving cars a ten-minute tune-up, or sticking the same microchip into the same place on identical circuit boards, over and over and over, a soul-nourishing experience at all. Such are the thrills of modern life.

Some people have few choices. Many of us have far more freedom of choice, when it comes to work, than we think we do, however. What do you value most, economic security or work that nourishes your soul? Are you willing to take some risks, stick your neck out, take a leap of faith? If so, then you can and will find work that nourishes your soul. You will.

What work do you want to do? Really. What must you do in order to do that kind of work and also pay the bills and buy the groceries?

5 ◆ *Listen to Music*

TIME WAS, in times gone by, music was either live or there was no music. Either you made music yourself, or you were present while others made music, or you didn't hear music. As simple as that. With the coming of recorded music and the radio, in the early twentieth century, all that changed. Now you can have music any time you want music. Tune in music on the radio. Put a vinyl LP, or an audio cassette, or a compact disc into the proper piece of playback technology, in your home or in your car, and you got yourself music at however many decibels you prefer.

Today we get music whether we want it or not. In the huge stores where we buy the stuff we buy we get music. Whether we want music or not. In elevators we get music, whether we want music or not. In the halls of the shopping malls we get music, whether we want music or not. Go to a park or camping ground, even, and you're likely to hear music coming from the portable music technology of complete strangers, and it may be music you do or do not like at a volume you may or may not appreciate. In our cars, without thinking, with a reflex movement of arm, hand, and fingers, we turn on the radio and get...music. Whether we want music or not. Did you decide you wanted music, or did you simply turn on the radio because it's there and you are used to having it on?

Music everywhere. Music on demand. Background music. But listen. How often do we actually listen to the music? How often? You can nourish your soul by listening to music, but you must *listen* to the music. Make no mistake about it, there is good music and bad music in all kinds of music. There is good rock music and bad classical music, good rap music and bad jazz, good folk music and bad reggae music. The only kind of music that has no bad music is Cajun music...but we won't quibble about that.

In order for music to nourish the soul, we must set aside all other activities and listen to the music. Listen to Mozart's "Requiem." Listen to Beethoven's "Ninth Symphony." Listen to music by a contemporary popular singer. Listen to the thought-provoking lyrics of singer/song writer John Stewart. Put on some Gregorian chant. Listen, just listen, maybe with your eyes closed. Listen to any music or song that communicates an intelligent idea...even if it's supposed to be funny. But listen, let the music fill your mind and heart. Don't try to think about anything else. Just listen. You may be amazed at what you hear.

Let the music fill your soul and nourish your soul.

6 ◆ *Learn a Poem By Heart*

PEOPLE who grew up during the first half of the twentieth century memorized everything from poetry to historical dates to prayers written by somebody else. Our grandparents and great-grandparents could complete Joyce Kilmer's poem, "I think that I shall never see..." They could recite lines from *Hamlet*, *Macbeth*, and *Romeo and Juliet*. But who memorizes anything today? Why bother? Put it in a book, and go read the book. Why memorize it? Put it on a computer disc and boot the computer if you want to "access" it. Why memorize anything? Why strain the brain when technological forms of memory can remember it for us? Why, indeed?

Memorize a poem you love and you'll discover why. Take up a volume of poetry. Find something not too long, say Robert Frost's "Stopping by Woods on a Snowy Evening." Memorize it line by line, first the first line, till you can say it by heart, then add the second line, then the third, until you can say the whole poem off by heart. "Whose woods these are I think I know. / His house is in the village though...."

A beautiful idea, that: "by heart." To memorize a poem is to know it no longer by vision from a page but...by heart. The poem is in your heart now, no longer merely on a printed page. You have it by heart, and when you know it by heart it's in your soul, as well, and your soul gathers nourishment from the beauty and truth the poem carries. "The woods are lovely, dark and deep. / But I have promises to keep...."

Now and then you come across a wonderful novel, and a line or passage in the novel is so delightful you want to keep it in your heart, so you learn it by heart. "It happened by the grace of God that Joseph Santangelo won his wife in a card game" (*Household Saints*, by Francine Prose).

"In Paradise, on the banks of the River of Time, the Lord of the Universe is playing ball with His archangels. Hundreds of spheres rest like white stones on the bottom of the river, and hundreds rise like bubbles from the water and fly to His hand that alone brings things to pass and gives them their true colors" (*Things Invisible to See*, by Nancy Willard).

"Active love is a harsh and dreadful thing compared to love in dreams" (Fyodor Dostoevsky, *The Brothers Karamazov*).

Discover your favorite poet and learn some of his or her poems by heart. Emily Dickinson. William Blake. It can be exhilarating to know a poem by heart, even a very short one: "The world will not be understood. / Put on a sword, put on a hood. / Listen. Can you hear me? Good. / The world will not be understood" ("Comedy," by Mark Van Doren).

The world bombards us with words all the day long, but few of them make it into our soul, thank God. When we learn beautiful words by heart they live in our soul with more truth and more beauty than was there before.

7 ◆ *Laugh until You Cry*

WE DON'T LAUGH with as much intensity as earlier generations did. We hear accounts of audiences sitting in darkened theaters watching movies filled with the antics of Laurel and Hardy, the Three Stooges, Abbott and Costello. People packed huge movie houses and watched the Marx Brothers, laughing uproariously, tears streaming down their faces. This kind of laughter doesn't happen anymore.

We see old Laurel and Hardy films today and smile. How simple, how quaint. Perhaps the old films evoke a chuckle now and then. But the effect isn't the same. We are more sophisticated than the people who first watched Stan and Ollie. People went wild with hilarity when they first witnessed Abbott and Costello's "Who's on first?" routine. Today, we smile maybe. Very amusing. But we don't laugh loud and long.

What can we do? Can we learn to laugh again as our grandparents and great-grandparents laughed until they cried? The great theologian Karl Rahner said that God laughs, so when we laugh we are more in touch with the spark of the divine that lives in us. By laughter, Rahner said, he did not mean the polite laughter of the highly "spiritual" person who is in complete control of himself or herself. "No, we mean real laughter, resounding laughter, the kind that makes a person double over and slap his thigh, the kind that brings tears to the eyes; the laughter that accompanies spicy jokes...."

When we hear about a book, movie, television program, play, newspaper column, or magazine article that is funny we should make an extra effort to find it and get the laughs to be found therein. We have our own funny men and women today, those with the ability to help us laugh at ourselves and the world. Sometimes entertainers today think they must be crude or in bad taste in order to make us laugh, but such entertainers don't last long. "The world is too serious," said political cartoonist Jeff Danziger, "not to laugh at it."

Laughter nourishes the soul when it is the outright laughter Karl Rahner described. Unfortunately, much of the humor we find today on television or in movies is more of a smirk and a wink than good, deep laughter that nourishes the soul. Television sitcom writers go way beyond Rahner's "spicy" jokes. Often, they don't seem to know how to evoke genuine laughter so they rely on the double entendre and one-liners that denigrate human sexuality. So where can we go for laughter that touches the soul?

Such laugher is a gift, and it comes as a surprise. The innocent malapropism or action of a child can do it. Sometimes even the old movies can still work their magic. The important thing is to be ready, open, innocent in your own heart as Stan and Ollie were innocent in their attempts to deal with an uncooperative world. Then the laughter will come, laughter that brings tears to your eyes.

8 ◆ *Look at Some Old Photographs*

VIDEO CAMERAS are popular today, just as an earlier generation thought 8mm movie cameras were the greatest. But neither video nor the old home movies are the same as photographs. Still photos we can hold in our hands. Transparencies ("slides") we can project on a screen. These capture a moment of time and hold it still for us so we can see the goodness and joy that was there. These enable us to see what we miss as time slips through our hands.

Take out the old photo albums and the shoe boxes filled with the old photos we never got around to putting in any particular order. Get out the disordered collection of slides, set up the projector, and drop the slides one by one into the carrier. Look at the old pictures. Here you are as you were. Here I am as I was. Here are the children as they were. Here are loved ones no longer living. Why couldn't we see how beautiful they were, and you were, and I was when we took these pictures? Why couldn't we see the goodness that was there?

You nourish your soul when you look at the old photographs because this helps you to see that the goodness and beauty that was there is equally real here and now. What was true then is still true today. All of us are lovable.

Nostalgia has a bad name. We think of it merely as a bittersweet longing for things, persons, or situations of the past. But if we return to the roots of the word we find a more positive perspective. Look it up. The word "nostalgia" comes from an Old High German word meaning "food for a journey" and a Greek word meaning "a return home." If we think of looking at the old photographs from these perspectives we see how this exercise can nourish the soul.

To look at the old photographs gives you "food for a journey," the journey of life, because it helps you to see that life is good now just as life was good then. We gather nourishment for the journey of life that you are still on, the pilgrimage of life. You "return home" to yourself by looking at the old photographs, home where the heart is. You renew your connection with your center. This is what's most important in life, the people you love.

9 ◆ Grow Older with Grace

I grow old...I grow old...
I shall wear the bottoms of my trousers rolled.
Shall I part my hair behind? Do I dare to eat a peach?
I shall wear white flannel trousers, and walk upon the beach.

THESE LINES from T. S. Eliot's "The Love Song of J. Alfred Prufrock" evoke both melancholy and a smile. It's as if the poet said: melancholy feelings are natural when we consider growing older, but let's not get maudlin about it; some people's attitudes toward aging are quite humorous, in fact. Growing older is natural and normal, after all.

Growing older is one of the facts of life, but our culture would rather not think about it. Oh, my. Growing older. We grow nervous thinking about it. We grow uneasy, for growing older raises questions about the meaning of it all. Growing older means gradual, irreversible deterioration. Ultimately, it means...death. Ack.

Truth to tell, growing older is a grace. Youth has its advantages and attractions, but think about it. Youth also has its drawbacks. Who would want to grow up again? Bummer. Who would want to cope again with the down sides of adolescence, school, getting a marriage onto solid ground, raising children — raising teenagers! — and launching them into the world? Growing older means looking back with some regrets, yes. Every life has regrets. But growing older is also the grace of looking back with satisfaction, more than a little relief, even. Certainly glad that's over with.

Growing older is a grace. It's the grace of knowing you did the best you could. You made some mistakes, yes. You even did some stupid things. But that's all in the past. It's all in the past. You have more past than you have future, and there's not a thing you can do about the past. Growing older is the grace of knowing that the present is all you have and it's all you need, all you will ever need.

Since growing older is a grace, grow older with grace. No whining, please, even when you must go to the doctor for a barium enema or go to the dentist to have a wayward wisdom tooth extracted. Even when you must go to the optometrist for bifocals...or *tri*focals! Do it all with grace. No whining. Do it with grace.

When you grow older with grace your soul grows younger by the day. That's the object of growing older, to cultivate a youthful soul. Young people have old souls, uncertain souls, frightened souls. Growing older with grace allows you to nourish a soul that has the shining eyes of a child, eager for life. Let your soul shine by growing older with grace. Life is an adventure. Let it shine.

10 ◆ *Write a Poem*

WHAT IS A POEM? A poem is words strung together in a manner calculated to pack the most meaning possible into the words you string together. Every syllable counts. A good poem is life concentrated into a package, and when you open the package it explodes with meaning and insight. A short poem says more than an essay on the same subject could say with ten times as many words. That's what a good poem is.

A poem can be about the most exalted or the most mundane experience. Take "This is Just to Say," by William Carlos Williams (1883–1963). In these delightfully simple lines the poet acknowledges to an unidentified person, his spouse, perhaps, that he has eaten some plums he found in the icebox, which "you were probably / saving" to eat for breakfast. He concludes:

> Forgive me
> they were so delicious
> so sweet
> and so cold.

Nourish your soul by writing a poem. Don't worry... and maybe give it some humor like Carl Sandburg (1878–1967) did in "Why Did the Children Put Beans in Their Ears?" First he asks why the children put beans in their ears "when the one thing we told the children / they must not do" was to put beans in their ears.

> Why did the children
> pour molasses on the cat
> when the one thing we told the children
> they must not do
> was pour molasses on the cat?

To write a poem is to call upon whatever is deepest in you, to call upon your soul itself to speak, however haltingly, however quietly. You give your soul carte blanche. Here, you say, here. What do you have to say, my soul? The process of putting words on paper, or on a computer monitor's glowing screen, is a process that cultivates the good soil of your soul as when you turn over the good soil of a garden. You turn over the soil, break up the clods, and aerate the ground so that good things may grow.

Write your own poem, even if you read it to nobody else. Write your own poem, and your soul will be nourished, will have more depth.

11 ◆ *Practice Meditation*

WE LIVE in a peculiar world. We dash about. Daily we dash about, and we fill our world with noises. Sometimes we call the noise "music," but usually it's "background music," and that's just another form of noise, something to throw a blanket over the silence. Something to help us avoid being in touch with our own deepest self, something to help us avoid awareness of... our soul.

This is what meditation is for, above all, to help us be open to hearing from our soul. Hello, soul? Are you there? I'm listening now. ... In meditation we give our soul a chance to whisper in our ear, to say something we may, just maybe, need to hear. Hello, soul? Come in, soul.

Meditation isn't difficult; meditation isn't an esoteric discipline reserved for Olympic athletes of the spiritual life. Meditation isn't for swamis and gurus alone; meditation isn't for strange characters from an esoteric land. Meditation is for everyone, and it isn't difficult. No need to let the idea make you nervous. It takes only a few minutes, and it takes only the desire to nourish your soul.

Can you find five minutes in your day? Five minutes you can set aside to waste some time on your soul? Five minutes when you can be alone? Five minutes when you can stop whirling and be still? Five minutes when you can be quiet? Once you find that five minutes, or make that five minutes, you're in business. The difficult part is over. What a relief. What a relief. The difficult part is over.

So here is your five minutes, your precious, golden five minutes. What will you do with your five minutes? Here is how you practice meditation. Ready? First, make yourself comfortable. This is crucial. Sit in a chair, or lie down on the floor, whatever, as long as you're in a comfortable position. Forget the lotus position. For the average North American person, just starting out, that's not comfortable. Now breathe. It's amazing how rarely we breathe in and out. So breathe in and out and pay attention to your breathing in and out. Do that for about thirty seconds.

Next, think of a word or a few words that put you in touch with your soul. "Love" may do it, or "God," or "Allah," or "Jesus," or "Ommm." The word doesn't matter in itself, since all words are but means to the same end, union with the Divine Mystery at the center of your own being.

Now, with your eyes closed, say the word silently to yourself, over and over slowly: "Love...Love...Love" or "God...God ...God..." Do this for five minutes. That's it. That's meditation. Do this once a day, every day for a month, and you will nourish your soul. You will become a more collected, more peaceful, more resilient person. You will.

12 ◆ *Play a Musical Instrument*

"**D**O YOU PLAY a musical instrument?" the questioner asks. "Yes," one replies. "I play the radio."

Yuk, yuk. So amusing. But not the same as playing a musical instrument. To play a musical instrument is to make music yourself, not listen to someone else make music. The latter is good, but the former is not to be missed. You don't need to be a virtuoso; all you need do is admit to yourself that it is possible for you to play a musical instrument. Repeat: "It is possible for me to play a musical instrument." Good.

Time is a problem, granted. But all you need do is locate five minutes when you can play a musical instrument, say two times a week. Got it? Got the five minutes? Great. Now, if you have a musical instrument you played at one time, would you like to play it again? If so, go ahead, get it out and play it...unless it was the piano and you don't have a piano now, in which case locating your instrument will be a bit more of a challenge....Brush up on your skills. You're all set.

Maybe you have never played a musical instrument, or maybe you have no interest in playing the instrument you once played. Fine. What instrument do you want to play? Are you willing and able to buy one and take lessons or teach yourself? Go ahead and do it.

Perhaps you don't want to buy a new instrument, or your budget won't allow that expense right now. No problem. Get yourself a jew's harp or a kazoo. These are musical instruments, too. You play for your own benefit only, nobody else need listen. Play away, make your own kind of music. What matters is that you make your own music, you don't listen to someone else make music, and you don't listen to a recording of someone else making music. You do it yourself.

There is the case of George Antheil, a twentieth-century American composer who early in his career wrote and performed avant-garde music that caused a sensation. Antheil's *Ballet mécanique* was scored for automobile horns, airplane propeller, fire siren, ten grand pianos, and other instruments. When it was performed at Carnegie Hall, a few minutes into the performance a concertgoer near the orchestra could stand no more. Tying his handkerchief to his cane, he raised a white flag.

Keep the sensibilities of others in mind. Be careful about playing an instrument that makes a bizarre sound, or music that people within hearing range may not be able to appreciate. If playing unconventional music, or an unconventional instrument, nourishes your soul, well, find a place away from others and play your heart out.

If you can't find an instrument that catches your fancy, don't give up. There is one musical instrument anyone can play. You whistle. You know how to whistle, don't you? You put your lips together, make a little "o" and blow. Whistle whatever you wish, from a simple tune to a symphony. That's playing a musical instrument, too. Play on.

13 ◆ *Enjoy Your Sexuality*

SOMETIMES we take our sexuality altogether too seriously. The Creator gave us our maleness or femaleness as part of the gift of being human. When was the last time you took some time to simply appreciate being a woman or being a man? Political issues related to being male or female are prominent, but sexuality is not fundamentally a political issue. It's a human issue. So nourish your soul by gaining a deeper appreciation for being a woman or a man.

If you are a man, what does that mean to you? If you are a woman, what does that mean to you? Don't think about the other sex, for now; just reflect on what it means to you to be whichever sex you are. Think about the times when you were most thankful to be a woman or a man. Why? Think about the times when you were most unhappy about being a woman or a man. Again, why?

Who are some prominent men or women who make you proud to be male or female? What do you admire about them? What have they taught you about being a woman or man?

Where do you think your feelings about being a man or woman come from? Most often we get our most basic feelings about our sexuality from our family of origin. Not only do we get our feelings about being a man or woman from our parents, but we get our feelings about sex in general from them. If we are comfortable about our sexuality and about sexual intercourse and sexual feelings, in large part we have our parents to thank. But the reverse is also true.

If you are married, cultivate your soul by talking about your sexuality with your spouse. Nothing is off limits. Talk about your feelings about being a man or woman. Talk about how you feel about sexual pleasure. Are you ambivalent about it? Why?

We live in a culture that, through the entertainment industry and mass market advertising, frequently trivializes sex. Either that or it presents images of maleness, femaleness, and sex divorced from reality. There is much to be said for the traditional conviction that sex belongs only in marriage. The divorce rate shoots up among couples who "live together" or are sexually active before marriage. It's true. Sometimes there is more to be said in favor of traditional sexual values than our culture gives them credit for.

Nourish your soul by facing up to any sexual prudery you may find in yourself. If you are married, make time to be naked with your spouse — naked physically but naked spiritually, as well. Let your bodily nakedness be a symbol for spiritual nakedness. Show your real selves to each other.

14 ◆ *Read a Good Book*

THERE IS NOTHING to compare with reading a good book if you want to nourish your soul. People flush so many hours down the toilet by gaping, slack-jawed, at television or video movies. There is a place for TV and movies, of course, but most of our TV and movie watching is the result of a bad habit, the result of mental laziness, the result of spiritual passivity. Reading requires us to become engaged with the printed word, to interact with what we're reading, to *think*. Thomas Edison said that most people would rather die than think.

Nourish your soul by reading a good book. If you're reading this, of course, you're reading a book, so maybe you don't need to be convinced. But perhaps you don't appreciate as deeply as you could the implications of what you're doing right now.

Reading is not just an enriching or entertaining activity. It can be a life-changing activity. Reading can lead you to change your way of life. Reading can teach you more than you bargained for. Reading can be a revolutionary or radical activity. You may be surprised.

Reading comes in two varieties, nonfiction and fiction, and each of these has many subcategories. Fiction includes short stories, novels, and science fiction, for example. Nonfiction includes everything from how-to books to books on spirituality such as this one. Both can nourish your soul, and both can change your life.

When was the last time a book changed your life? Different books do it for different people. You set out to nourish your soul and find your life changing instead. There are some books that bear reading more than once. Take *Walden,* by Henry David Thoreau. This is a book you should read once when you're young, again in middle age, and again when you are old. Each time you read it, at each stage of life, you'll find different insights that touch your heart and nourish your soul. On the topic at hand, for example, Thoreau wrote:

No wonder that Alexander carried the Iliad with him on his expeditions in a precious casket. A written word is the choicest of relics. It is something at once more intimate with us and more universal than any other work of art. It is the work of art nearest to life itself. It may be translated into every language, and not only be read but actually breathed from all human lips; — not be represented on canvas or in marble only, but be carved out of the breath of life itself....

How many a man has dated a new era in his life from the reading of a book. The book exists for us perchance which will explain our miracles and reveal new ones. The at present unutterable things we may find somewhere uttered.

There are books without number, of course, and many of them are good. But to nourish your soul read not just the good but the best.

15 ◆ *Spend Time in Quiet Solitude*

T HOSE OF US who inhabit the so-called developed nations also
live in what is called "mass culture." This means, among
other things, that we are conditioned from our earliest days to
seek out the crowd. We are uncomfortable with the idea of solitude. We grow restless at the very idea of being alone and quiet.
Silence is enough to drive us batty. But what a loss this is. For
in silence and solitude you discover yourself and establish your
own integrity.

Early in the twentieth century a young Swiss physician, Max
Picard, grew disillusioned with the practice of medicine, disappointed that in the big hospitals patients were being treated as
objects instead of as persons. It was as if they existed for the
sake of medical science instead of the other way around. Picard
left medicine and studied philosophy. Then he moved to the little village of Caslano, Switzerland, where he spent virtually the
remainder of his long life reflecting on the conditions human beings had to cope with in modern societies. His two best-known
books are *The Flight from God* and *The World of Silence*.

In *The World of Silence* Max Picard wrote:

> Silence is nothing merely negative; it is not the mere silence of speech.
> It is a positive, a complete world in itself.
>
> Silence has greatness simply because it is. It *is*, and that is its
> greatness, its pure existence.
>
> There is no beginning to silence and no end; it seems to have its
> origins in the time when everything was still pure Being. It is like
> uncreated, everlasting Being....
>
> Silence contains everything within itself. It is not waiting for any-
> thing; it is always wholly present in itself and it completely fills out the
> space in which it appears....
>
> Silence is the only phenomenon today that is "useless." It does not
> fit into the world of profit and utility; it simply *is*. It seems to have no
> other purpose; it cannot be exploited.

To spend time in silence and solitude — even if only a few
minutes a day — is to open yourself to the truth of your own
existence. Are you ready to face the deepest truth about yourself?
Many are not. The truth may be too frightening, too contrary to
commonly accepted assumptions about the meaning of life, the
universe, oneself, and others.

In silence and solitude sooner or later we come face to face with the most basic human questions. The spiritual traditions of the West — Judaism and Christianity — have more to say about this on a deep level than seekers sometimes give them credit for. They say that we are created by God, the Divine Mystery. We are here to love our Creator and one another. And we are destined for final union with our Creator.

16 ◆ *Keep a Journal*

HAND-IN-HAND with spending time in silence and solitude comes the practice of keeping a journal. Nourish your soul by keeping a journal. No need to be fancy about it. Any old spiral-bound notebook will serve. Record your thoughts. Write down what occurs to you. When you write a poem, put it in your journal. When you read a book and find a passage that impresses you, copy it down in your journal; make your own collection of quotations from many sources.

Your thoughts and ideas are your own. When you write them down in your journal, they take shape outside of you where you can look at them and evaluate what you are thinking. Does this make sense? Is it really a good idea? Write it down, then read it a few days later. Do you still think this is true? Watch your thoughts and feelings develop by writing them in your journal.

Keep a journal as a record of your journey or pilgrimage from day to day, week to week, year to year. You are not the same person today that you were five or ten years ago. Look back, read your old journals from days gone by. Nourish your soul by evoking memories of where you have been and all that you experienced. There is no nourishment for the soul like cultivating memories.

Call it nostalgia. "Nostalgia" has something of a bad name. People scoff at the idea of "indulging in nostalgia." But look. To feel nostalgic can be nothing more than a bittersweet longing for the past. But it can also be a source of nourishment for the journey into the future.

The past is not just a source of romantic feeling. We may

want to be in touch with our past for the sake of moving into our future in better ways. Or we may be determined to not leave our past entirely behind because we may find in our past valuable resources for the future. We do not want to forget our past or indulge in the foolish fantasy that we can separate ourselves entirely from our past. Rather, we carry our past with us, and the past can help us learn how to shape the future in better ways.

To keep a journal is to collect our own nostalgia as food for our journey in life. We write in our journal trying to better understand the past and the present. We read past entries in our journal for insight into how to live today and tomorrow. Thus do you nourish your soul.

To keep a journal daily is a discipline, however. It requires that you make time for quiet, solitary reflection, at least a few minutes each day.

17 ♦ *Cultivate Your Marriage*

SOMETIMES we take for granted everything that is most familiar. Indeed, there is an old saying: "Familiarity breeds contempt." If you are married, a primary source of nourishment for your soul is your marriage. Would you believe? Imagine that. Your spouse, good old Frumpkin, is a key to your spiritual vitality, your union with the Great Cosmic Wherewithal.

Nourish your soul by renewing your intimacy with your spouse. It can be done, no matter how long it has been. Assuming you have a basically healthy marriage, simply bring it up. See here, Frumpkin, I would like to feel closer to you, more in touch with the Great Cosmic Wherewithal present in our relationship. What say you? Eh?

Recite some wry and witty T. S. Eliot to him or her, your eyes half-closed, your voice husky, perhaps sex on your mind, and pause between lines to chuckle:

> Let us go then, you and I,
> When the evening is spread out against the sky
> Like a patient etherised upon a table;
> Let us go, through certain half-deserted streets,
> The muttering retreat

Of restless nights in one-night cheap hotels
And sawdust restaurants with oyster-shells....

Or something more romantic might be more suitable. Either way, poetry can bring a spark of vitality and wit if recited at an unexpected moment. Have some fun together, laugh together. That's the ticket.

If you are married, your soul and the soul of your spouse overlap with each other, they blend like the weave of a hand-woven fabric. Your souls do. So to nourish your soul is to nourish the soul of your spouse, and to nourish your marriage is to nourish your soul and the soul of your husband or wife. There is a mystery here....

Nourish your soul by cherishing your marriage. Make efforts to overcome the familiarity that breeds contempt. Don't take your spouse for granted. We all do it, we take our spouse for granted, but stop it, resist the inclination. To take your spouse for granted, your marriage for granted, is to let weeds grow up through the weave in the shared fabric of your shared soul.

Touch the tip of your nose to the tip of your spouse's nose. Say the magic words of love: "Woochie-woochie-woochie!" Then kiss your spouse on the tip of his or her nose. Twice.

Or: do something completely unexpected for your spouse. If you are a man, make the beds. Or bring home flowers. If you are a woman, tell him to do something he enjoys that you ordinarily are not enthusiastic about him doing. Or surprise him with wild, uninhibited sex on your mind.

18 ◆ *Trust the Great Cosmic Wherewithal*

WE ARE SO READY to be afraid. We are so inclined to anxiety. Something bad is going to happen. If the future is unclear, it's best to be pessimistic. This is the way.

We find it difficult to trust in anything except money, for in our culture money is the ultimate source of security. So. Nourish your soul by placing your trust in a greater reality: God, the Creator, our Father in heaven, Allah, the Great Cosmic Wherewithal, your Higher Power, Whoever. Place your trust in the benevolence of the Ultimate Reality. Whatever metaphor works for you. Trust in God as a loving God who loves and cares not just in general but...for *you*.

Sit down, lie down, whatever position is most comfortable. Be there. Be quiet. Be calm. Be open. Be. Pay no attention to your usual anxieties. Don't resist them or get in a fight with them. Just ignore your fear of what might happen. Call upon God as a loving God who loves and cares for you. No matter how bad things look, call upon this God who loves you with an infinite love. Breathe evenly, calmly. Ask this loving God to help with whatever fear or anxiety you have. Just ask. Then wait. Quietly wait. Wait quietly. Breathe evenly, calmly. Be.

Even if the world is not entirely benevolent, ultimately life is benevolent and the universe is kind. The Ground of All Being wants your peace and good, and your problems and anxieties will work themselves out. Do what you can, do all that you can, then stop. God is at work in all that you do, bringing all things to good for you. It's true. Trust in the love and benevolence of the Great Cosmic Wherewithal.

The kindness of God is an ultimate kind of kindness. It is a benevolence that is stronger than death, even stronger than death. Even if you face what appears to be an ultimate kind of darkness — death — the kindness of God is more powerful than that. If you have reason to believe that you will die from a terminal illness, you probably will. All the more reason to trust in the goodness and kindness of the Ultimate Ground of All Being. All the more reason to abandon yourself to a loving and compassionate God. All the more reason.

We all die, so we all face this choice: to trust in the ultimate benevolence of the Darkness we are moving into, believing that on the other side of the Darkness there is unimaginable Light. When you trust in the ultimate benevolence of the Darkness, you begin to see the Light, and feel its warmth, even this side of the Darkness. Trust in the Light.

Nourish your soul, no matter what kind of life you have now, no matter what troubles you face. Nourish your soul by trusting. Trust is all.

19 ◆ *Sing a Song*

IT's EASY to sing, or hum a tune at least, when you're feeling happy and at peace. Which is great. But sometimes we don't think about singing a song when we're down. Feeling blue? Singin' them down-home, tail draggin' blues? Stand up. Think of a song you like. Down and dirty or sweet and long. Fill your lungs with air and sing that song.

We are embodied spirits. When we do something bodily we do something spiritually. So sing that song to nourish your soul. Think of your song as a prayer, no matter what kind of song it is. We have too narrow a perspective on prayer. Prayer happens any time the soul reaches out beyond itself to seek Something More. So sing your song as a prayer from your soul. Sing it. Let loose and belt it out, or sing it, wing it, filling in the places where you forget the lyrics with dum-dee-dum, la, la, la. . . .

You don't need to be in the shower to sing. Sing where you are. Sing in your car, sing on the street. Especially if you don't think you have much of a voice, can't carry a tune in a bucket, especially then: sing. Who said you can't sing? Even if you don't have a great voice you can sing. Anyone can sing. Just do it. Sing. Whoever said you can't sing told you a lie. Open up your mouth and let 'er rip. Sing it.

You think *you* can't sing, hey, there have been some great entertainers who couldn't sing but sang anyway. They paid no attention to the people who told them they couldn't sing. Fooey on other people's standards. You may not have a conventional singing voice, but you have your own unique *style*. So use it.

The great comedian and singer Jimmy Durante showed us all how. He sang in spite of a terrible voice. He once recorded a duet with the great opera diva Helen Traubel. Together they sang "The Song's Gotta Come from the Heart," and it became a Victor Red Seal record, high-class stuff. Helen Traubel said to Durante: "It's a pleasure to record with a great *artiste* whose voice sounds the same with bad needles."

You can sing, I can sing, all God's children can sing. So nourish your soul by singing a song. Once a day, at least, sing yourself a song from the heart. If you don't like singing alone, play a recording you like and sing along. Sing a duet with one of your favorite singers, and let it come from the heart. Let 'er rip.

Especially if things are looking bleak, sing a song. Yes, things are looking bleak. Don't deny it. But sing a song all the same. It can't hurt, and it can help you cope, help you trust, help you. It can. Sing a song from the heart about how unhappy — or happy — you are. Rat own.

20 ◆ *Visit a Museum*

SOME PEOPLE think of museums as boring places, boring, boring, dull. Not so. A good museum is a place to wake up. To nourish your soul. Even small towns often have little historical museums, collections of this, that, and whatnot from the past that say something to us about who we are. Bigger cities almost always have one or more museums — art museums, historical museums, museums dedicated to everything from airplanes and space exploration to teapots and doll houses.

Nourish your soul. Muse in a museum. Betake yourself to a museum and see what you see. Muse on the remarkables you find there. Let the remarkables sink in and nourish your soul. Ponder the ponderables and let them nourish your sense of wonder, awe, or perplexity. Let modern art puzzle or surprise and delight you. Let art from past centuries raise questions in your mind. What? Why? Where? Who? Let the questions pop like tiny firecrackers in your mind. Pop! Bang!

Stroll through a museum with nothing on your mind. Find a painting or sculpture that touches something in your heart. Sit down in front of it and look. Just look. Don't try to analyze. Just look. Let it overwhelm you. Drink it all in until you are full. Don't try to figure it out. Just look at all the details and the whole piece of art. Let the colors and textures swim into your mind. Let the art nourish your soul in secret ways, ways you can't begin to think about. Just look.

If you're standing in a small-town museum, no great works of art to be seen, only artifacts from days gone by, pay attention. Look. There in the old photographs. The faces. Those were real people, as real as you are now. Young faces, old faces. Men standing near a house, women standing near a fountain in a park. What do the faces in the old photographs say to you? What do they say? Listen.

Touch the rusted old farm tool. Run your fingers over the rough surface of the old implement, the smooth surface of the old table, the cracked leather of the old black bag once carried by a country doctor. Let the textures into your heart, let the old faces touch your soul, let the faded colors speak to you in whispers. Listen. Whispers.

You travel to a large city to a famous museum. Great works of art by the greatest artists. You stand in front of a famous aircraft from the days when human flight was new. You look. Nourish your soul. What does the old airplane say to you? What does the old space capsule say to you? What is the message of the huge old airplane that flew but once, never again? Touch the wild mix of colors in the hand-blown glass, feel how smooth it is. Nourish your soul. Wake up.

21 ◆ *Give Away Something You Cherish*

SOMETIMES it's difficult to tell whether we own things or they own us. Consider home ownership, for example. Do we own the house or does the house own us? Do we own the car or does the car own us? You sign on the dotted line thus obligating yourself to make payments each month. You give up some of your freedom so you may own a house or car.

If you want to maintain ownership you must make the payments, and to make the payments you must work every day, perhaps at a job you're not happy with. If you want to move someplace else or merely go on a two-week vacation, you must make arrangements for someone to keep an eye on the house to discourage would-be burglars. You must hire someone to water the lawn and mow it in your absence. While you are away, you may worry about your house. Is everything secure? Is the lawn being watered and mowed? Do you own the house or does the house own you?

Ideally, you should be able to own things rather than them owning you. But this takes spiritual liberty, a deep sense that you control the things you own, they don't control you. One way to cultivate this liberty of soul is to give things away now and then. Sure, you may give away things you no longer want, worn out things, things you no longer use or care about. But the key here is to give away things you still cherish.

There is a traditional Native American perspective that views a gift as more valuable depending on the number of times someone gave it to someone else. Thus, if you give someone a gift five other people already gave, and it's a truly wonderful gift, it becomes a gift all the more laden with value. You may borrow something of this attitude when it comes to giving away things that you cherish.

The idea is to give away something you cherish but can certainly live without. You need your house to live in and your car for transportation, but look at how many other cherished things you own. Pick and choose, pick and choose, then find one of your cherished possessions to give away. Perhaps you have a book that means a great deal to you. You cherish this book, you have read it many times. Perhaps now it is time to give it to someone else who will cherish it in turn. Your soul will be nourished if you give it away.

Think of anything you own that gives you much pleasure or satisfaction — a particular recording of a particular piece of music, perhaps, or a painting or framed photograph. Give it to someone who will cherish it as much as you do and enjoy it just as much. You enjoyed it for years; now it is someone else's turn to enjoy it. So make of this cherished possession a gift, a gift from the heart. Doing so will nourish your soul.

22 ◆ *Belong to a Believing Community*

THERE IS a popular attitude which views membership in a formal worshiping community as a stuffy, old-fashioned, even phoney thing to do. "Everyone knows" that people who take "organized religion" seriously are hypocrites, weak people who can't look life straight in the eye. They need "organized religion" as a crutch. Why don't they just grow up and leave spiritual infantilism behind?

There may be more to membership in a traditional religious community than this, however. What would you say is easier, faith or skepticism? Is it easier to believe or to disbelieve? Skepticism and disbelief are simple, as easy as pie. It's the easiest thing in the world to claim agnosticism. It's the easiest thing in the world to claim belief in God but want nothing to do with "organized religion." After all, the truly fashionable people in our culture see no need for "organized religion," so why should you?

There are so many reasons to reject "organized religion." Such groups seem so filled with squabbling over doctrinal issues or issues related to formal worship practices. Why bother, even if you do believe in God? Why not simply worship God in your own way and ignore "organized religion"?

This line of thought seems to make sense, and countless people agree with it. Trouble is, it overlooks something crucial. Actually, it's rather naive. Easy skepticism, easy disbelief, make no demands on us at all. It's easy to adopt such a position and go on living merely for appearances' sake, self-centered and superficial as always.

Participation in the life of a believing community requires that you leave self-centeredness behind. Therefore, it nourishes your soul. Participation in the life of a believing community makes demands on you that you would never have to face were you to wander through life with little on your mind but yourself. In a believing community you can't say by the way you live, "Go away and leave me alone." The community is always there, irritating and demanding as it can be, constantly prodding you to leave selfishness behind, constantly nourishing your soul in ways you would never think of on your own.

Formal worship plugs you into a living religious tradition and makes it impossible to forget that countless others came before you and countless others will come after you. You do not belong to the ultimate human generation. You find yourself praying as your great-grandparents prayed and as your great-grandchildren will pray long after you cross over the Great Divide. And, oh, how this nourishes your soul.

23 ◆ *Breathe In and Out*

SOMETIMES the simplest, most ordinary activities can nourish your soul. Take breathing, for example. We do this all the time, in and out, in and out. But how often do you breathe in and out with awareness? How often do you think about what you're doing?

Sometimes we don't breathe well. Oxygen deprivation. We become preoccupied with our work, preoccupied with worry and anxiety, preoccupied with doing so we forget about being. So nourish your soul by breathing with awareness. Sit down. Calm down. Now breathe in and out, slowly. Listen to the air as it enters and leaves your lungs. Ask yourself: What does this mean?

Here is what it means. It means the most obvious yet the most wonderful thing in the world. It means that you are alive. You are alive! Breathe in and out, slowly, and know that you are alive. What a wonder. What a quiet, spectacular, amazing wonder. You are alive, breathing in and out. Imagine that. Just imagine it.

Breathe slowly, in and out. There are prayer methods based on awareness of breathing in and out. Breathe slowly in. Say a short prayer as you do. Breathe slowly out. Say a short prayer as you do. Over and over, over and over. The most natural prayer in the world. Breathing in and out....

Now and then, wherever you are, become aware of your breathing in and out. Become conscious of your breathing. Focus on breathing in and out. It nourishes your soul. Think about breathing. This is the difference between life and death. If you are alive, you breathe in and out. If you are dead, you do not. So be alive. Breathe naturally, with quiet, with calm. Say thank you for the gift of breathing in and out. Say thank you for the gift of life.

Life and breathing in and out cannot be separated. To breathe is to nourish your soul, so breathe now and then with awareness of the life that breathing makes possible. The Book of Genesis identifies breath and life with each other, as if breathing is itself life. God says: "And to every beast of the earth, and to every bird of the air, and to everything that creeps on the earth, everything that has the breath of life, I have given every green plant for food" (1:30).

So ponder this, that when you breathe you take in life itself. Breath is life, life is breath. Nourish your soul by breathing in and out. Yet how insubstantial breath is. A breath is almost nothing, yet it makes the difference between being alive and not being alive. Is this not a wonder? Think about this and nourish your soul.

24 ◆ *Take a Day Off*

FRANTIC. Sometimes our days seem frantic. We whirl through our days, whirl through our weeks and months. Many people become so attached to work-related activities that they hardly have a life apart from their work. They forget that for a life to be worth living one should work in order to live, not live in order to work.

Nourish your soul. Take a day off. Call in "sick" if you can't get the day off any other way. Don't work for one whole day that would ordinarily be a work day. Don't work. Goof off all the day long. Sleep much later than you ordinarily would. Enjoy a long soak in the tub. Do nothing productive or practical. Wander around aimlessly. Take an aimless walk in a park. Treat yourself to a lunch you can't afford. Eat ice cream or, if it's not summer, drink hot chocolate. Read a good book. If you are married, try to take a day off together.

There are some things you should *not* do on a day off. Do not think about work. Do not catch up on work from the office. Do not watch television all day. Do not clean house. Do not feel guilty about taking a day off.

Use your day off in useless ways. Putter about. Go for a bicycle ride, go skiing, or drive into the countryside for no particular reason. If it's raining, watch the rain. If it's snowing, watch the snow. Stare out the window at nothing in particular. Daydream. Choose five of the ways to nourish your soul in this book and do them all on your day off.

A day off nourishes your soul because it is a time to stop acting as if everything is in your control. Everything is not in your control, but no need to be anxious about that. Ultimately, everything is not in your control. What a relief. It's best to do your best and then trust in God who does care about you and your seemingly insignificant little life.

Taking a day off is a declaration of independence. See here, world. I am who I am, I am not what I do. See here. See here. If all you do is stand there, breathing in and out, you have tremendous value simply because you are a human being. Take a day off to remind yourself of this. In the long run, you are free from the demands and expectations of a myopic world.

In the long run, you will die. Take a day off to remind yourself of this. Don't be morbid; that's not the point. The point is that along will come a day when you will have to turn loose of everything whether you want to or not. So take a day off to let go. Let the world spin away without you, let the wheels turn without your assistance for one day.

Nourish your soul. Take a day off. Just enjoy being.

25 ◆ *Write a Letter to an Old Friend*

YOU HAVE a friend from days gone by, someone you still feel close to, but you haven't had much contact. You could call your old friend; the telephone is a marvelous device. But writing a letter would say much more. There is something about a letter, something about the written word that says that you care more than a phone call would. So write your old friend a letter. Type if you like, or use a computer. Some think e-mail will rescue the written word. Regardless of your chosen method, write. Write a letter to an old friend. It will nourish your soul and the soul of your old friend.

Bring your old friend up to date. Write about the big and little events in your life since you last had contact with your friend. Write about whatever comes into your head. Write about your joys and concerns. If you are married write about your spouse. If you have children write about them. But don't forget to write about yourself, as well. Write about what's in your heart. Write about your work. Write about your hopes and dreams. Write about your disappointments. Write about a thing or two you learned since last you saw your old friend.

Do you have mutual friends, your old friend and you? Write about them, too. Have you seen some of them more recently than your friend? Write about them. Write about days gone by, hopes fulfilled or disappointed from the old days. What are you grateful for? What do you not understand about life and the world even after all these years?

Put your thoughts down, write them down. Get them out there on paper for your friend to read. Try, however, to avoid using clichés. Your friend does not want to read that time has been flying or that much water has passed under the bridge. He or she already knows this, thank you very much.

Groucho Marx despised the empty clichés of business correspondence. A letter from his banker ended with the standard phrase, "If I can be of any service to you, do not hesitate to call on me." Groucho immediately replied by letter: "The best thing you can do to be of service to me is to steal some money from the account of one of your richer clients and credit it to mine."

Don't limit your letter to telling your friend about events in your life. Write, too, about your thoughts and feelings. Talk about religion, politics, and whatever else stirs you up these days. Let your friend know who you are now, not just who you were years ago. Fill your letter with personal observations on life, the world, and the meaning of it all.

Make your letter to an old friend a long one.

26 ◆ Read a Book You Wouldn't Ordinarily Read

WHEN YOU READ a book, chances are you choose that book because it is the kind of book you like to read. The topic of the book is interesting to you. You enjoy gardening so you are ready to read a new book on gardening. Or perhaps you enjoy any book by a particular author. You are a fan of James Lee Burke, or Annie Dillard, or Jon Hassler, or Anne Tyler, or Mary Higgins

Clark, so you read new books by your favorite author as they appear. Certainly books on a favorite topic or by a favorite author nourish your soul.

To not only nourish but stretch your soul, read a book you wouldn't ordinarily read. You have no great curiosity about the history of Minnesota, so read a book on the history of Minnesota. You are not intrigued by religions other than your own, so read a book on other religions. Here is the truth: you can learn more about what you already know by reading about people, places, or things you know little or nothing about.

You can learn more about Christianity by reading about Judaism or Islam. You can stretch your soul by reading a book by a historian of religion. You can nourish your soul by reading a book by an author you never heard of before. You can nourish your soul by reading a book by an author you are sure you'll disagree with.

Perhaps you don't take fiction seriously. Maybe you think of fiction as a mere diversion to be taken along only on summer vacations. Maybe you think of fiction as less important than nonfiction. Are you ever mistaken. Read some great fiction and you'll find out why. Read a classic, such as *Silas Marner*, by George Eliot, or a contemporary classic, such as *Franny and Zooey*, by J. D. Salinger. Read *Half-Wits*, a wonderful but little-known novel by Gerard Goggins about the mystery of good and evil. Good fiction nourishes the soul like nonfiction never will.

Next time you visit your local public library, instead of heading for the usual sections you gravitate toward, consciously choose to browse in a section you rarely visit. If you almost never read history, wander through the history section. If you hardly ever visit the nonfiction area, go there and see what you can find. Browse the books on astronomy, business, or the care and feeding of gerbils. Read a biography of a person you never heard of before.

We all too often allow ourselves to drift in the same old directions, the same old patterns, and it's good for the soul to purposely bump yourself into a completely different groove now and then. Otherwise we become spiritually stale.

27 ◆ *Watch a Laurel and Hardy Movie*

P ROBABLY you have heard about people who turned up with a
terminal illness and decided to respond not only with medical science but with humor. People have laughed themselves
back to health, and one of the ways they laugh is by watching
old movies starring Laurel and Hardy, the Three Stooges, Char-
lie Chaplin, Buster Keaton, the Marx Brothers, or Abbott and
Costello. The old comedies have something newer cinematic approaches to comedy do not, and whatever it is it makes people
laugh and laugh.

Laughter nourishes the soul. Laughter is one of the most appropriate responses to the human comedy. If we can laugh, long
and hard, it means we don't take ourselves or the world too seriously. It means that we know, deep inside, that appearances to
the contrary ultimately everything will be okay. Ultimately, life
and the universe are benevolent, and God is in love with us and
all of creation.

Why do the old comedy films nourish the soul in special
ways? It's difficult to pin down, but they actually seem to have
a spiritual quality about them. Stan Laurel and Oliver Hardy,
in particular, revealed a remarkable degree of insight into the
simple joy and goodness of living. No matter what happened,
they retained a kind of innocence of heart unique to their approach to humor. In his biography *Mr. Laurel and Mr. Hardy,*
John McCabe observed:

> Laurel and Hardy lasted twenty-nine years (1926–55) as an active work-
> ing team, and yet in all that time their basic gags were not many and
> they remained the same. Clearly, then, there is a deep, basic quality —
> dare one call it spiritual? — that kept them in public affection for so
> long, a quality transcending the mere oddity of physical appearance, pan-
> tomimic ability, and gag cleverness. This element permeated their work
> and it is inherently their brightest glory. The quality is *innocence.*

In a 1928 two-reeler titled *Leave 'Em Laughing,* there is a
scene where Stan and Ollie, still under the influence of "laughing gas" after a riotous visit to the dentist, cause a major traffic
jam in their topless Model T Ford. Stopped by a cop, played by
Edgar Kennedy, Stan and Ollie laugh uncontrollably, and before
it's over the cop has lost his pants.

In a still from this movie, Stan and Ollie sit in their flivver laughing and laughing as the cop, in his long johns, writes them out a ticket. This scene is a wonderful image of a healthy spirituality. Stan and Ollie laugh uproariously as the cop scribbles on his pad. But the cop, grim as he can be, has no pants. Stan and Ollie stand for a healthy spirituality that refuses to take religious legalism (the cop) seriously. Laurel and Hardy represent the soul set free and watching their films helps set us free too.

28 ◆ *Give Up Bitterness*

IT'S EASY to advise someone to give up a negative, hopeless, bitter outlook on life, and sometimes the advice is deserved. In other cases, people are so deprived of power and control over their own lives that they become bitter and resentful at a young age and stay that way. It's the extraordinary individual who can overcome social and cultural circumstances to become a confident, hopeful member of society.

This said, it's amazing how often people in ordinary circumstances take refuge in bitterness and resentment. "I can't" is their theme song. "I can't. I have no power, no influence, no ability to improve my situation. And it's not my fault. Poor me."

Nearly everyone slips into this pathetic state now and then. To nourish your soul, give it up. Give up bitterness and resentment. They do no good, not for you and not for anyone else. All they do is render you powerless. Bitterness and resentment eat away at your soul, eroding your energy, depleting your natural reserves of talent and inspiration.

Give up bitterness. So the world done you wrong. Big deal. It happens to everyone. Don't feel like the Lone Ranger. Whatever you are bitter and resentful about happened yesterday, or last week, or years ago. Forget it and move on.

Sometimes people become dedicated whiners. They blame their present unfortunate circumstances on others. "I'm unhappy because my parents didn't give me healthy self-esteem." "I'm depressed because my father beat me, my mother ignored me, and my brothers and sisters hated me. It's all their fault." "I'm addicted to nicotine and alcohol because I had an unhappy childhood. It's not my fault."

People who talk like this are sitting ducks for self-help gurus who charge enormous fees to attend their workshops. "Find your inner child," they beckon, "and you will be free and happy again." "Gotta find my inner child," the guru's groupies purr. They romanticize the idea of childhood. They forget that sometimes children are the most obnoxious beings in the world — almost as obnoxious as adults sometimes are.

Bitterness and resentment are understandable. Bad things happen to good people, and good people don't like it one bit. Why should such bad things happen to me? But look. Life is a mix of good and bad, happy and sad. You have to expect that sometimes life will kick sand in your face. So what? Pick yourself up, dust yourself off, and get back to living. So things didn't work out the way you hoped they would. All the same, you can try something else.

Give up bitterness and resentment. It will nourish your soul.

29 ◆ *Visit Someone Who Is Lonely*

DOROTHY PARKER (1893–1967) was a famous short-story writer, theater critic, and writer of light verse. She was also a wit, and she used her wit to advantage one time when she was lonely. Parker had a small, drab, cubbyhole of an office in the Metropolitan Opera House building in New York. The trouble was, no one ever came to see her. So when a man arrived to paint Dorothy Parker's name on her office door, she talked him into painting, instead, the word "gentlemen."

Not everyone has the opportunity to deal with loneliness the way Dorothy Parker did. Anyone who is house-bound will tell you that there is little a person in such circumstances can do except wait and hope someone will come to visit. Lonely people need to have people visit them, but what we sometimes don't realize is the extent to which visiting someone who is lonely can nourish your soul.

What is loneliness but the absence of human companionship?

What is easier to give someone than your presence? The surprising thing is how nourishing such visits can be for your own soul. Indeed, if you are lonely one of the best things you can do is to visit someone else who is lonely. That way you nourish two souls with one visit.

Where can you find someone who is lonely to visit? It's not difficult, not difficult at all. In convalescent homes, retirement facilities, day care centers, the place you work, down the street, just around the corner you will find lonely people. The tough part is not finding a lonely person to visit. The tough part is deciding to visit a lonely person in the first place. You're so busy, you have so many things to do. But look. Your soul needs the opportunity to visit someone who is lonely and you hardly realize it. At all, at all.

Fine, you say. I will visit someone who is lonely. My spirituality requires it, my soul needs it, and — more important — the lonely person needs it. So I find a lonely person. It's not difficult. I go to visit. What do I say? What do I do?

Here is what you say and do: nothing. Quite often, a lonely person wants nothing more than someone to listen, someone to show some care. A lonely person is still a person, the same person he or she has always been. So get to know the person you are visiting, even if it is your own elderly mother, father, aunt, uncle, or cousin. Get to know the person you are visiting. Ask what his or her life has been like. What is the person interested in now? People don't stop being alive when they're lonely, so find out what the person likes to do.

Once you get yourself off the dime, visiting a lonely person is easy.

30 ◆ Be a Kind and Considerate Driver

DRIVING an automobile can be dangerous to your soul. Or at least it can deprive you of the peace of mind and heart you had before you got behind the steering wheel. What is it about driving? A well-mannered person, a person who ordinarily is as polite as can be, can turn into a mean-spirited, ill-mannered, profanity-spouting pain in the neck for other drivers once he or she is on the road. Freeway driving seems to be especially dangerous. In the late 1980s, on a few occasions drivers actually started shooting guns at one another on a Los Angeles freeway, and a couple of people died.

Perhaps it's the psychology of driving a car that does it. You are in control of a large machine, a machine with tremendous power, a machine that is also a status symbol. Roar, roar, roar. You *become* your car. How dare anyone be rude to you on the road? Another driver stops suddenly and you almost have a collision. Anger surges through your entire being. Maybe you shout an obscenity at him or her or make an obscene gesture. He or she does the same in return. A few blocks down the street you see your chance to get even. You rev your engine as you wait at a stop light, and when the light changes to green you roar away from the intersection and get ahead of the other driver.

You drove around the block three times looking for a parking space. Suddenly you spot one. You step on the gas wanting to get that parking space before another driver sees it. Just as you are about to pull into the space, another car whips around your car and zips into the parking space. You're furious. It was obvious you were about to park there.

To nourish your soul, you can plot and plan to be a kind and considerate driver. Instead of giving in to anger, instead of being a driver who shouts obscenities and makes obscene gestures at the slightest perception of offense, you can give way to other drivers and be patient when they make stupid or unsafe choices.

You and another driver spy the same empty parking space at the same moment and make a dash for it, arriving at almost the same moment. As a kind and considerate driver, you may give way to the other driver. So you actually got there first. Big deal. The world will go on. Gesture kindly and smile as you back your car away and allow the other vehicle to park. You'll feel good for having made such a choice.

Think of driving as a way to express your true self, not of the automobile as a powerful extension of your desire to be in control. Think of your driver-self as the same as your regular-self. Be just as polite in your car as you are at other times. It will nourish your soul.

31 ◆ *Look at Your Hands for Five Minutes*

SERGEI RACHMANINOFF was a great Russian composer, pianist, and conductor. After the Russian revolution of 1917, he lived mainly in the United States. During a concert tour in 1943, Rachmaninoff became ill and was admitted to a hospital in Los Angeles where doctors told him he had cancer. Knowing that he was dying, the great pianist looked at his hands and murmured, "My dear hands. Farewell, my poor hands."

Nourish your soul by looking at your hands for five minutes. We take our hands for granted, yet they do so much for us. Think about a typical hour in your day. What would that hour be like without your hands or if your hands were damaged so you couldn't use them as you ordinarily do? Your life would be different, very different, without your hands. So look at them and appreciate all they do for you.

You work with your hands, of course. You hold your fork and knife with your hands when you eat. When you were an infant and young child you probably drew comfort from sucking your thumb. You use your hands to take a bath or shower, to keep yourself clean. Try shampooing your hair without your hands. With your hands you drive a car, shake hands with a friend or new acquaintance, and make love to your spouse. Your hands make it possible to open a book and turn the pages as you read, turn on a television set, and push the buttons on the remote control.

We communicate with our hands, as well. Try speaking with your hands tied behind your back. Gestures we make with our hands are an underappreciated part of our conversations. People who are deaf use their hands to communicate with sign language.

Our hands are an important part of who we are; they are not just instruments we use. We do not only good things with our hands but, sometimes, bad things. People steal with their hands and do violence to others with their hands. Boxers put padded gloves on their hands before pounding each other at length. Dancers dance with gestures of their hands and arms as much as with their legs.

Our hands grow and change with us throughout life. Think of your hands when you were a child, a teenager, a young adult.

What do your hands look and feel like now? What will they look like ten years from now? Think of all your hands have done for you, on request. Do you play the piano, the trumpet, the clarinet, the harp, or another musical instrument with your hands? Do you tend a garden with your hands? Tap the keys on a typewriter or computer keyboard?

Nourish your soul. Look at your hands. Meditate upon your hands and all they do for you. Give thanks for your hands.

32 ◆ *Think about Your Children*

PARENTHOOD is one of life's most rewarding and most challenging experiences. No one who has not been a parent can fully appreciate all that parents know and feel. The heart of a parent no longer belongs to him or her. Someone once said that once you become a parent your heart is no longer within you; it is always outside you wherever your child may be. To become a parent is to open yourself to the deepest joys and the most intense anguish a human being can know.

Think about your children, no matter their ages. Nourish your soul by thinking about your children, each one. Think about your child's infancy, early childhood, childhood, and adolescence. Are some of the later stages still in the future, or are they all in the past? What have you learned from your child?

Children make adults of their parents. How did your children help you to grow up? How have they nourished your soul for, lo, these many years? Think about it. Nourish your soul. Think about it.

Parents come to their children's defense out of love. When Harry Truman was in the White House, in 1950, his daughter Margaret gave a public singing recital in Washington, D.C. Paul Hume, the music critic for the *Washington Post*, wrote afterward that Margaret's voice had "little size and fair quality." He said that she sang flat much of the time and complained that there were "few moments...when one can relax and feel confident that she will make her goal, which is the end of the song."

The president angrily replied in a letter to the critic: "I have just read your lousy review buried in the back pages. You sound like a frustrated old man who never made a success, an eight-ulcer man on a four-ulcer job, and all four ulcers working. I have never met you, but if I do you'll need a new nose and plenty of beefsteak...Westbrook Pegler, a guttersnipe, is a gentleman compared to you. You can take that as more of an insult than as a reflection on your ancestry."

This letter was made public, and most Americans seem to have approved of Truman's fatherly readiness to jump to his daughter's defense. As might we all in similar circumstances.

Consider the mystery that each child is from the moment of his or her birth. But consider, too, that your child is a regular human being with faults and strong points unique to him or her. Do you sometimes feel guilty for failing as a parent, at least in some respects? What's done is done, and each child is a person in his or her own right. Each one is free, makes choices parents have no control over, and will live his or her own life. Parental guilt is frequently unjustified.

33 ◆ Be Open to Possible Miracles

THE GREAT French novelist Anatole France won the 1921 Nobel Prize for literature, but his work was frequently marked by a deep vein of pessimism. Visiting Lourdes, the novelist looked around at all the crutches, canes, and similar equipment left behind by people apparently cured after prayers for healing at the famous shrine. He remarked, "Don't see any wooden legs."

Anatole France had a narrow view of miracles. For him, a miracle required that a missing leg be replaced with a whole new leg. Otherwise, he would explain away the possibility of miracles using one of the 101 methods any skeptic has ready at the drop of a hat.

Expect miracles when the outlook looks most bleak, if for no other reason than the fact that miracles are so common. Nourish your soul by being open to the possibility of miracles. Albert Einstein put it this way: "There are only two ways to live your life. One is as though nothing is a miracle. There other is as if everything is."

That's the point, of course. Everything is a miracle, but we are so used to seeing miracles all the time that we don't think of them as miracles. What nincompoops we are! Let's begin at the beginning. Consider, if you will, the miracle of your own existence. Did you bring yourself into being? Hardly. Your parents were involved, of course, but they were mere accidental participants. Ask any parent about the birth of a child. It's a miracle. Parents have much less control over who their children will become than they or the parenting experts would like to think. Your parents had nothing to do with the essence of your utterly unique identity. Where did that come from? It's a miracle, of course.

Consider the miracle of your continued existence. Do you keep yourself alive? Do you will your heart to go on softly pounding in your chest? What makes it happen? It's a miracle. When you go to sleep at night, why do you wake up in the morning? It's a miracle. Why do you breathe in and out all night while you're asleep? It's a miracle, no matter what technical explanation science may have. In the long run science observes, it doesn't explain why.

See that tiny little acorn? Hold it in your hand and say, "This will grow into a huge oak tree." It's hilariously funny when you think about it. It's so funny that it's a miracle because it's true. Stand in the middle of winter snow and ice and say, "All this will be green and warm in a couple of months." Who could predict it based on immediate evidence alone? Knock yourself out laughing! It's a miracle!

You are a miracle, and your life is a miracle.

34 ◆ Prepare a Wonderful Dinner at Home

SIDLE UP to your parents or grandparents. Ask them about eating in restaurants when they were children. They will tell you that eating in restaurants when they were children was a rare and special occasion. There was no such thing as "fast food." No golden arches, no pizza delivery person knocking on the door.

Mealtime was home time. Maybe once in a blue moon the family would eat in a restaurant, maybe while traveling. That's the way it was for most people, anyway.

Today, the average person "eats out" several times a week, and it's not unusual for the experience to happen in a "fast food" restaurant. Line 'em up, get the burgers, fries, and drinks on the trays, collect the money, and do it all over again. We take it for granted. It's the modern way of life.

Nourish your soul. Take the time to prepare a wonderful meal at home. Make it special. Take hours to prepare special recipes, special dishes, special sauces. Use fresh ingredients, make the vegetables delicious with a special touch. The main course can be both simple and glorious, both tasty and beautiful to look at. Spread a nice tablecloth and put candles on the table. Gather friends. Serve special beverages. Make it special, every part of it. Let it become a ritual. Pray before you eat, raising everyone's awareness of the sacred character of what you are about to do.

A special meal with people you love. Nothing can be more sacred. For to eat together is more than to eat together. To share a special meal is to nourish not just bodies but souls. How rarely we take the time and trouble to do this. It need not be a holiday. Do it to celebrate the holiness of the ordinary. Invite people to join you for no reason in particular. Tell them it's a celebration of nothing and everything.

A special meal prepared at home is not so much a meal as an opportunity to enjoy and ritualize the goodness of being alive and of having family and friends. We say to one another around the table that we are bound to one another by a mystery that transcends appearances. Even when we are apart we are together because we are a family or we are friends. This is no merely formal affair; it is a statement of fact and mystery.

To invite your boss and his or her spouse to dinner is a formality. To have a dinner with people you genuinely love is a sacred activity with roots in the Divine Mystery. So let there be no formalities for the sake of appearances, only efforts to make everything special as a sign of the love that you share.

Nourish your soul by the meal that you prepare and share.

35 ◆ *Get a Physical Check-Up*

NOURISH YOUR SOUL by getting a physical examination? What? What? What kind of suggestion is this? Recall that you are not just a soul riding around in a body. Your soul does not ride around in your body much as you climb into a car, airplane, or train. You *are* your body; you are an *embodied spirit*. Therefore, it makes perfectly good spiritual sense to have a regular checkup from a physician.

A physical exam reminds us just how bodily we are, and how in-process we are. The doctor listens to your heart, checks your blood pressure, zeros in on your eyes, ears, nose, and throat. He or she taps your knee with a little hard rubber mallet, and your leg jumps a little. Whack. (Jump.) Whack. (Jump.) A blood test will be done. Women know the joy of the pelvic exam, men the joy of testicular and prostate exams. If you have a family history of colon cancer, the doctor may think it prudent to include special exams with this in mind. Ah, the thrill of the barium enema and the sigmoidoscope or colonoscope.

To get a complete physical checkup is to admit to yourself that you are mortal, subject to the same aging processes as the rest of humankind, subject to illness and disease. Better to be humble about it. Chances are the results of your physical exam will all be positive. Say hey, you're still perking along just fine. If the doctor finds something that needs attention, well, it's time to deal with it. That's a spiritual process, too, just like health is. What's the impact on your soul? How will your spirituality come into play here? If you are an embodied spirit, illness or disease affects your soul as much as your body. Address it....

To be alive is to change, and to be a changing human being is to be growing older. This becomes clear as the years go by. Perhaps the doctor says that your cholesterol level is too high and you need to do something about that. Cut down on fatty foods, cut down on red meat, eat more grains and vegetables. Fewer burgers and fries, more salads. In other words, change your lifestyle, get healthier. Life is about making choices, and some of the popular options out there are not the best ones, no matter how much we like rich ice cream, chocolate, and fried chicken.

Healthier choices about how you eat are healthier choices for your soul, as well. Imagine that. As embodied spirits, our eating habits reflect and shape our spirituality. If you sit around all day watching soap operas and eating bon-bons, that's a spiritual issue as much as a physical one. If you rarely exercise, that has an impact on your entire being, embodied soul that you are. Give it some thought.

Nourish your soul. Get a physical exam.

36 ◆ *Become a Prayerful Person*

P RAYER is simpler and more complicated that we often think it is. There is a wonderful passage in a wonderful novel, *Reservation Blues,* by Sherman Alexie. The story's central characters are young Native Americans living on a reservation in Washington state. The main character, whose name is Thomas Builds-the-Fire, walks outdoors one night, under the stars:

> "Hello," he said to the night sky. He wanted to say the first word of a prayer or a joke. A prayer and a joke often sound alike on the reservation.
>
> "Help," he said to the ground. He knew the words to a million songs: Indian, European, African, Mexican, Asian. He sang "Stairway to Heaven" in four different languages but never knew where that staircase stood. He sang the same Indian songs continually but never sang them correctly. He wanted to make his guitar sound like a waterfall, like a spear striking salmon, but his guitar only sounded like a guitar. He wanted the songs, the stories, to save everybody.
>
> "Father," he said to the crickets, who carried their own songs to worry about.

The prayer of Thomas Builds-the-Fire is basic, honest, open, and direct. His prayer is the prayer of his heart. Thomas Builds-the-Fire is a teacher of prayer and honesty.

The best prayers are the most honest prayers. So nourish your soul by praying, but pray from your heart, not from your head. Look at a tree. Say, "Help." Look up at the stars in the night sky. Say, "Ah" or "Oh." Stand naked before a full-length mirror and say, "Thank you." Stand there until you can say it and mean it.

This may strike you as perplexing, but there are times when the most honest prayer in the world may take the form of language you almost never use — profanity, swearing, four-letter words. Look at something you think is ugly, a blight on the landscape, say. Tell the Divine Mystery how you feel about it. "From your lips to God's ears," goes the old Jewish saying.

Nourish your soul by talking with someone else about prayer. Tell a friend what you think about prayer. Be honest. When do you pray? Why? Do you pray only in "holy" situations or circumstances? Or do you pray where prayer is most appropriate, in the midst of your ordinary life? Do you pray about cleaning the house, earning a living, paying the bills? Do you pray in the middle of a pelvic or prostate exam? These are fine times to be aware of the presence of the Divine Mystery at the core of your being. Pray not in words but with a sigh, a prayerful sigh.

Be aware of your constant communion with your Creator, who loves you with an unconditional love, any time at all. Tell God a joke — as long as your joke is not about a priest, a minister, and a rabbi. Please.

37 ◆ *Be Generous to the Point of Extravagance*

HAVE YOU EVER had a fantasy about what you would do if you won a state lottery or inherited several million dollars? Chances are your fantasy included giving away some of your new fortune. But look. You don't need to wait until you win the lottery to know the thrill of extravagant generosity. It can happen now. Nourish your soul by giving away some money, even if it's not a huge amount.

How much money would you spend on an evening out and think nothing about it? Good. Skip the evening out, just this once, and give that amount of money to someone you know who could use it for essentials. Give it to the last person in the world you can think of who would expect to receive money. Put the cash in an envelope and put it in a place where that person will find it. Don't tell him or her the money came from you. Just watch the person's eyes light up.

If you want to be extravagantly generous with your time rather than your money, find a single parent and offer to take care of the kids so she or he can have a day off. Or join Big Brothers/Big Sisters and spend time regularly with a child who needs an adult in his or her life. Volunteer to teach an adult to read; illiteracy is more widespread than you might think. Opportunities to volunteer are almost endless, and there's a place for you. Volunteer and you will nourish your soul.

Being extravagantly generous with your time or money is good. But think of this: you can be extravagant with your love for the people you are most likely to take for granted. Always. Nourish your soul by being more available to a child when you could have a successful career instead. Not that the two are mutually exclusive, but sometimes we need to ask ourselves about our priorities. Is it most important to give our children money and possessions or ourselves?

When Paul Tsongas was a U.S. senator from Massachusetts, he decided not to seek a second term because he wanted to spend more time with his wife and children. At the press conference where he announced this decision he said, "No man ever said on his death bed, 'I wish I had spent more time at the office.'"

Sometimes being extravagant with our love for those we love requires some sacrifices. Do you base your decision on what the world values most or on what you value most? Do you put personal values first or material values first? How can you balance the two? How can you be generous to the point of extravagance with your love?

Your soul is nourished by giving, and what matters most is that you give of yourself, even when you give money.

38 ◆ *Take a Walk*

CHARLES DICKENS had a daily schedule. He was always in his study by 8 a.m., where he wrote until noon. At this point his wife brought him his lunch, which he ate at his desk. He returned to work until 2 p.m., at which time he left home and took a thirteen-mile walk through the English countryside. In the evening he spent half an hour with his children — who eventually numbered ten — prior to retiring for the evening.

It's the thirteen-mile walk we may find particularly note-worthy. Imagine taking a thirteen-mile walk each day. On his walks, Dickens often strolled through little towns and villages, taking in the details of the houses and people. Because he had a great memory for details, he could retain much of what he saw and would later use it in the story he was writing.

Walking is not just physical exercise or a way to get from one place to another. Walking can also nourish the soul in unique ways if you walk not just with your legs but with your mind, heart, and soul. Walking and praying go together well, too. The key is to walk with your senses open and your intellect attuned to what you observe as your walk.

A young man walked each evening one mile away from his home and one mile back again. He looked at the houses he passed, at the trees, the occasional airplane overhead, and the changes in the seasons as they showed themselves in nature around him. The young man walked day in, day out, for years, at the end of each day. Then one spring evening as he returned from his walk he paused on the corner across from the house where he lived with his wife and young children. He looked at the house, struck by a completely new realization.

It suddenly hit the young man that his walk gave him a unique point of view on his life. Ordinarily when he left his house he was in his car, driving, and departures and arrivals happened ex-peditiously, without much thought. Walking, however, he paused upon his return, struck by the knowledge that in that house was everything he held most dear, his wife and children. There they were, the children asleep, his wife sitting quietly in the living room strumming her guitar, humming some old tune, tired after a full day. The young man murmured a thank you to no one in particular and to the wide and starry universe and the Creator of it all.

A walk can be a deeply spiritual exercise, deeply nourishing to your soul if you want it to be. The key is to walk but not think about the walking. Be in touch, instead, with your surroundings as you walk. Be in touch, instead, with your deeper self as your walk. Don't strain, don't make a mighty effort. Simply relax and let it be so.

A walk of this kind is nourishing to your soul. Imagine that.

39 ◆ *Accept Praise*

WE TEND to have an unbalanced notion of how to respond when someone gives us praise or a compliment. We deflect the kind remark with false humility. "No big deal." "Oh, well...." "Anybody could have done it." "It's not that important." "I didn't do that much, really."

Oliver Wendell Holmes, Sr., a great nineteenth-century writer, physician, and professor of anatomy and physiology at Harvard University, loved flattery. Even when he was in old age, Holmes encouraged people to flatter him, using his hardness of hearing to that end. "I am a trifle deaf, you know," he would say to someone who had just praised his latest literary work. "Do you mind repeating that a little louder?"

The term "humility" is related to the Latin *homo*, human being. To be humble is to accept yourself as human, no more and no less. When you do a good job, or excel in some manner, it's less than human to deny that you used your gifts or talents well. The humble person doesn't grovel; the humble person accepts praise or compliments without depending upon them in the future. The humble person stands upright without acting like a stuffed shirt or getting a big head.

Of all the great novels and stories he wrote, Charles Dickens's favorite, the one that held a special place in his heart, was *David Copperfield*. One of the characters in this novel is the despicable, hypocritical Uriah Heep, who defrauds his employer and has designs to marry his daughter and thus take complete control of his employer's law practice. Heep constantly writhes in the presence of others, bowing and groveling with false humility. He regularly insists that he is "very 'umble," but his humility is a mask, a way to ingratiate himself with those he wishes to control.

Uriah Heep is the exact opposite of the truly humble person. Genuine humility will nourish your soul because it inclines you to acknowledge the truth about yourself, no more and no less. If you play the piano well, you don't scoff at the enthusiasm of others for your playing. If you have a gift for writing poetry, you don't pretend you have no such gift. You accept the encouragement and kind remarks of others and do what you can to cultivate your gift.

If you see a house ablaze and run into the house and save its occupants, you don't deny that you showed bravery when the media folks show up to put you on television and in the newspapers. You admit that you did save those people's lives, but you don't act as if you're pretty hot stuff, by golly. When the mayor gives you an award at a special banquet in your honor you accept the award, make a few remarks about the importance of smoke detectors, and then go home and get on with your life.

40 ◆ *Do the Right Thing*

S AY YOU'RE WALKING in a shopping mall. You glance down, and there before you on the floor is a ten-dollar bill. It's not a huge amount of money, but obviously someone dropped it by accident. You pick up the money and glance around. No one seems to be looking for lost money. You glance to your right and see a little gift shop. What next? What's the right thing to do?

You can stuff the ten-spot in your pocket and keep on walking. No one will notice. The person who lost the money may not miss it until he or she gets home. On the other hand, it could have been lost by a child or teenager who needs the money for lunch or transportation home. Without it what will he or she do?

This series of events actually happened to a real person. Without formulating the question in exactly these terms, the person who found the ten dollars wanted to do the thing that would nourish her soul. So, she went into the little gift shop, explained what had happened, and left her business card. "If anyone comes in looking for a lost ten-dollar bill," she said, "here is my phone number. Have the person call me and I'll return the money."

The little and big ethical choices you make either nourish your soul or deprive it of life. It's up to you to do the right thing. If you lie to protect yourself you deprive your soul of nourishment. If you tell the truth even though it means admitting that you did something wrong you nourish your soul. It's a paradox. "The truth will set you free."

You're at work and hear a fellow employee giving vent to racist or sexist attitudes. Do you keep quiet or quietly but firmly speak up for justice and truth for all, regardless of race or sex? Do you want to let more light into your soul or let it slip back a little into the shadows? You can speak up for goodness and truth in a manner that sidesteps self-righteousness. You can speak up for equal treatment for all, and that will nourish your soul.

You have a chance to sneak into a baseball game without paying for a ticket, and your children are with you. Do you go ahead and sneak in without paying, or do you do the right thing? Do you say by your actions, "Cheat when you can get away with it," thus darkening your soul. Or do you make it clear that you're not interested in cheating and then go ahead a buy tickets like everyone else?

No matter what, do the right thing. Not only does this nourish your soul but it helps others to make good choices as well, thus helping them to nourish their souls too.

41 ◆ *Listen to Your Heartbeat*

LISTEN to your heartbeat. Listen. Listen. You are alive. You are a remarkable fact, a complete truth, an evident reality, a living and breathing human being. Listen to your heartbeat. You are alive. But listen to your heartbeat. Your heart softly pounding in your chest. Nourish your soul by listening. You must be quiet in order to listen to your heartbeat, so be quiet and listen. Listen.

Your heart pumps blood through your entire system, ka-whump, ka-whump, ka-whump.... Your heart beats in your chest efficiently. But what keeps it going? Do you will it to keep on thumping in your chest? No. It just happens. It just happens. But does anything "just happen"? No. Everything must have a cause. What causes your heart to keep on beating in your chest?

Someone versed in physiology would tell you that your heart is a muscle about the size of your fist that beats about seventy times a minute and more than a hundred thousand times in a single day. Your heart pumps five quarts of blood through its chambers every sixty seconds and does enough work in one hour to lift a weight of one and-a-half short tons more than one foot off the ground. The right side of your heart takes impure blood containing carbon dioxide from your body and pumps it to your lungs. The left side collects pure, oxygen-rich blood from your lungs and pumps it to your body....

And so on and so forth. *But what made your heart start beating before you were born, and what keeps it beating now?* Ah, that's the mystery, that's the mystery. We may describe the physiology of the heart and the various processes that characterize its functions until yon cows come home, but we still will not have answered this question.

Only your heart — meaning now the center of your being, not a part of your anatomy — can tell you what keeps your heart thumping in your chest. Only your heart. It speaks a deep mystery into the silence of the mystery of your own being. It says that only your heart can tell you the answer to this question, but the answer is freely available for the asking, for the small and simple asking of the question. So ask....

Listen to your heart softly pounding in your chest. It pumps the blood, but what does the sound of your heart say? Does it speak? Does it speak to you? If you close your eyes, sit quietly, and listen, your heart will speak to you. It may say something like this: *God's love... God's love... God's love.* If you listen, your heart may speak these words to you, or something like them. Something very like them.

Your heartbeat speaks a mystery of love. Listen.

42 ◆ *Visit a Zoo*

THRONGS OF PEOPLE visit zoos every year. Families are big on zoos, parents with children in tow, walking from display to display. Parents pushing babies in strollers, parents carrying babies in backpack carriers. Older children dash from one creature to another, exclaiming about this and that. People stand on this side of the fence watching the elephants, tigers, bears, gorillas, and giraffes. They stand outside the cages watching the monkeys. They peer over the edge into the huge pool where the seals fly through the water performing their natural antics; they peer into the water as the otters swim on their backs making otter sounds, slapping their wet bodies into the water over and over again.

Nourish your soul by visiting a zoo? Indeed. What do you find in the zoo besides the creatures large and small, swimming and walking, flying and leaping? You find connections between yourself and the rest of creation, that's what you find, and these connections can nourish your soul.

Watch the zebras or the angel fish. What do they have to do with you? Are they curiosities only? Do varieties of marvel populate the earth to keep us humans amused only? No, not just that. Surely they are entertaining and a marvel. But the countless other-than-human beings on the earth have value and importance in themselves. Indeed, we have more in common with them than not. More in common than not. For we are all a part of creation, all with a special place, a special goodness and beauty.

We might ask where the other-than-human beings fit in. Where do they fit in? But that question means, Where do they fit in with us? We might also ask, Where do *we* fit in? Which means: Where do we fit in with *them*? Where do we belong on the earth in relation to the whales and lizards and parrots, the creatures in the zoo? Where do *we* fit in? Good question. Answer that question for yourself, and live your answer, and your answer will nourish your soul.

We human beings are, first of all, part of creation right along with the creatures in the zoo. We put them in the cages, the confined spaces, but the purpose of the zoo is fulfilled only if we go and come home feeling more a part of all that we saw there. St. Francis of Assisi got it right more than seven hundred years ago: Brother Wolf, Sister Bird. In the final analysis, when it all shakes out, it's not us and them; it's only "us," all of God's creatures together.

There is nothing but joy when we claim our kinship with God's other creatures: Brother Elephant, Sister Seal. It nourishes the soul.

BETTER to light one candle than to curse the darkness, goes the old adage. If you feel like cursing the darkness in your life or in your soul, light a candle. You could do worse, and you may find that it helps. You may. It could nourish your soul.

Maybe you're feeling good, down-home, God's in heaven (right here) and all is right with the world. It's a cold winter's night or a warm summer evening. Light a candle as a symbol of the light in your life right now. It could nourish your soul.

A lighted candle is a powerful symbol that can function in all kinds of ways. Do you feel lonely? Light a candle. Do you feel distant from God? Light a candle. Do you find it impossible to pray or meditate? Light a candle. A lighted candle is a symbol of prayer and worship. It's a sign of a light that transcends any light you'll ever see with any eyes but the eyes of your soul.

Any time is a good time to light a candle. When it's time for a meal light a candle in the middle of the table to remind you that the Creator gives you the food to nourish your body as well as all that you need to nourish your soul. If you share your meal with others let the candle remind you that in your sharing you meet more than a need for physical nourishment; you meet a need to nourish one another spiritually, as well.

To light a candle is a simple thing to do, a small thing to do. But it can be such a comfort. Is a child frightened by a storm? Light a candle and read a poem about something mysterious and beautiful and simple. Is a child unable to sleep because he or she is afraid of the dark? Light a candle across the room that you'll extinguish later after sleep has come. Tell the child about the candle. Pray a simple prayer about angels and billowy clouds and the comforts of love. Is the child upset or the baby fussy for no reason you can discover? Light a candle. It will nourish the baby's soul and your soul, too.

Several centuries ago in Ireland the English tried to suppress Catholicism by persecutions. Priests had to visit homes at night to say Mass in secret. During the Christmas season Catholic families left their doors unlocked and put lighted candles in the window to guide priests to their homes. English soldiers noticing the lit candles and open doors were told that it was to welcome

Mary and Joseph on Christmas Eve. The soldiers dismissed it as harmless superstition, and the signal of the lighted candles remained.

A lighted candle can touch the heart and nourish the soul when nothing else will do the job. Nothing else.

44 ◆ *Get Socially Involved*

THOSE INCLINED to spirituality sometimes slip into the attitude that one's spirituality is a personal matter that has no social dynamic. Are they ever mistaken. Any authentic spirituality related to any Western religious tradition, if you check into it, has a clear thrust toward the wider society. Spirituality isn't just the Divine Mystery and you off in a cozy corner by yourselves. That's called spiritual narcissism.

Nothing will nourish your soul like serving other people who have special needs. Nothing will nourish your soul like regular time spent working in a soup kitchen, or helping the homeless, or volunteering some time to work with mentally handicapped people or children who are hospitalized. Nothing.

Ask anyone with any experience. They will tell you that serving others who have special needs does good for the ones you serve. But it does more good for you. It's a mystery. Feed the hungry and you feed your own soul. There is nothing as important as this. Judaism and Christianity have some basic differences, but they both have their mystical traditions, too. They both have a thrust toward serving one's neighbor. Islam, too, is neighbor-oriented and compassionate. Something there is in the human soul that needs to reach out to the needs of others. Something.

In each human being there is a spark of the divine, and this spark seeks its own kind in others. You might say that this is why we are here, knocking elbows on planet earth, in order to care for one another. So when you live for others you fulfill something deep in yourself. When you live for yourself, live for only yourself with nobody else in mind, center on your own self-centered wants and desires, then you gravitate toward meaninglessness and the void.

Let there be in your life a regular time and place in which you place not just some money but yourself, your body and soul, at the service of others. It's easy to send money to worthy causes, and that's good. But think of the former television sitcom celebrity, plenty of money in retirement, who goes once a week to a place for homeless men. There she picks up a large laundry bag of men's socks with holes in them. She repairs the socks and launders them in her own home. The next week she returns the laundry bag filled with wearable clean socks and picks up another bag filled with socks that need to be repaired and laundered.

This has been going on for years. The former celebrity hasn't done a thing to rid the world of any big-time social problems. She simply meets the need of some homeless men for clean socks with no holes in them.

45 ◆ Forgive Someone Who Did You Some Wrong

AFTER SEVERAL YEARS of living apart, Dorothy Parker, a great twentieth-century American writer, reconciled with and remarried her second husband, Alan Campbell. At the reception following the wedding she remarked, "People who haven't spoken to each other for years are on speaking terms again today — including the bride and groom."

You know the stories. Members of the same family haven't spoken to one another for many years. Both sides refuse to budge. No one will say, "I'm sorry." So the estrangement goes on and on. Endlessly, perhaps. On and on. You may not be involved in something exactly like this, but you may know someone who was a friend but is no longer. A former friend now alienated from you and you from him or her. Hard feelings, a hurt that still festers after all these years. Neither of you has been willing to reconcile.

Nourish your soul. Take the first step. Or if the other person has tried to reconcile but you have refused, now is the time.

There is in your soul a wound that will not heal until you and your friend forgive each other and patch things up. Bury the hatchet. Neither of you will live forever, and there is no time like the present to make a present to each other of a friendship reborn.

The eighteenth-century English poet William Blake wrote that "we are put on earth a little space, / That we may learn to bear the beams of love." With these words Blake implied that sometimes, at least, love is not easy, may even be painful. This applies to times when forgiveness is called for, forgiveness on your part for someone who wronged you, hurt you, did something to you that, until now, you found unforgivable. Forgiveness is called for to nourish your soul, help your soul to regain a health it hasn't known for so long.

So long bitterness, so long hardness of heart. Bye-bye emptiness, hello fullness of heart and compassionate forgiveness. It is the better part, so let it be. Screw up your courage, set your hat right on your head, and get in touch with the person who wronged you, hurt you, did something to you that you found unforgivable. Reach out. Can either of you even remember what the estrangement was about? No matter, the time for forgiveness and reconciliation is now because now is the only time you have.

Forgive and by forgiveness you will learn to bear a little more the beams of love, the love that nourishes your soul above all things. No matter what the matter may be, seek to forgive and seek reconciliation. There is no hurt, no wrong, that cannot be forgiven. Nourish your soul.

46 ◆ *Make a List of the Times It All Worked Out Fine*

S IT DOWN. Sit down and make a list. Pick up a pen or pencil, and sit down with a sheet of paper to make a list. Try to think of all the times disaster seemed imminent. Try to think of all the times. Write down all those times the future looked bleak but the worst that you feared did not happen. Make a list of all the times when everything worked out fine. No disaster. Make a list of all the times, you might say, that God delivered when you prayed for help but you were mostly relieved and maybe thought about being grateful to God for no more than a minute or two. Think about all those times and make a list.

No matter how many times God delivers, the Divine Mystery comes through for us, we respond to each new crisis, as it looms on the horizon, as if God is not to be trusted. No matter how many times we were spared disaster in the past, or brought through disaster into a good place on the other side, we still feel and act as if the Great Cosmic Wherewithal is indifferent toward us, at best, or out to get us, at worst.

This is where traditional metaphors for God and attributes and images of God deserve some attention. You can think about these and what they mean, for these traditional metaphors, attributes, and images carry countless centuries of human experience — human experience of the Divine Mystery — in their pockets.

Islam tells us that "God is kind and beneficent." The Hebrew Scriptures present a "living" God, a God who is Life itself, a God who is at once radically near to His people and utterly transcendent. The Christian Scriptures highlight God as "Father," a metaphor that carries a meaning closer to "Loving Papa." Postscriptural Christian tradition also sets before us a God who is a loving Mother. All of the traditional images, divine attributes, and metaphors have one thing in common: they insist over and over that God cares for us, loves us more than we can imagine, and is completely trustworthy.

No matter how much grief and pain you may be able to identify in your life so far, on the other side of the darkness you will find light. No matter how many times disaster seemed just around the bend, you will see that God has never allowed you to face more than you could cope with. Many times when the future looked dangerous and threatening it turned out to be a safe harbor, after all. Yet on each new occasion you find it difficult to trust in God's love for you. You find it difficult. We all find it difficult. So make a list. Make a list to nourish your soul.

Our religious traditions tell us that the Divine Mystery is loving and kind. Our own past experience tells us that God is trustworthy. So trust.

47 ◆ *Spend Time with a Child*

ADULTS SOMETIMES romanticize childhood. Children often have a difficult life, what with being knocked around by adults, victimized by politicians who use them as pawns on the chessboard of their careers, teachers who don't really enjoy being teachers, inner city violence, homelessness, and parents who try to live their lives through their children. Childhood and adolescence can be difficult, and many adults would have to admit that they would not want to go through it all again.

All the same, children are sometimes more in touch with the truth than adults, and an excellent way to nourish your soul is to spend time with a child. Set aside the solemn importance of all that you do in the so-called adult world and spend some time with a child. Do what the child wants to do. Thus you will find yourself spending time in ways you never would choose for yourself. You may find yourself doing things that seem foolish. You may find yourself.

A young child will invite you to get down on the floor and play. A young child will ask you to push her in a swing or watch ants crawl up the side of a tree. A child will ask you to go for a ride on a carousel or eat an ice cream cone. A child will take you for rides on escalators, up and down, up and down, and a child will take you to a baseball game or ask you to play basketball one-on-one. A child will ask for a hug and give you a hug in return. A child will laugh right out loud and make you laugh too.

Nourish your soul. Do all of these things.

Hans Christian Andersen, the great nineteenth-century Danish writer of fairy tales, discussed the march for his funeral with the musician who was to compose it. "Most of the people who will walk after me will be children," Andersen said, "so make the beat keep time with little steps."

A child will do this for you. He or she will make you slow down and take little steps. Walking with a child you will find that you must walk more like a child walks, not getting there by a direct route, perhaps, sometimes running, sometimes walking slowly. A child walks for the sake of walking; an adult walks to accomplish some goal, usually in a hurry.

A child will ask you to read the same story aloud over and

over. You may put yourself to sleep doing this, which is okay. A child will ask you to play video games you might not be inclined to play. Play them anyway, and ask questions as you go. A child will ask you to pretend. So pretend as if it were real. A child will ask you to use your imagination, and a child will take you to a movie where you will eat popcorn and giggle.

Nourish your soul. Spend time with a child being childlike.

48 ◆ *Lock Yourself in Your Room*

SAY YOU'RE FEELING DOWN, bluesy more or less. Say you're feeling discouraged and defeated. Say someone has hurt your feelings, disappointed you, or caused you to question your own value. Say you are feeling rather worthless. Say you are bored. The root of your problem is forgetfulness. You have forgotten something important.

This may sound like a strange idea, but do it anyway to nourish your soul. Lock yourself in a comfortable room — a bedroom, say — and vow not to leave that room until you remember what you forgot and feel significantly different. Vow not to leave that room until you remember right down to your toes that you are loved by God with an absolutely unconditional love. Vow not to leave that room until you *feel* this love in the center of your being.

Good move. Don't expect instant results, however. This could take a few hours. So bring nourishment with you, but no junk food allowed. Bring fresh fruits, a few fresh carrots, some pure water. Bring a loaf of whole grain bread or some whole grain rolls. Bring food that is loaded with nutrition, no empty calories, no heavy-duty fat content. Bring food for your soul into your locked room.

Now sit down or lie down. If you lie down and go to sleep, that's good. If you go to sleep that's because you need the rest, body and soul. Don't fight it. If you sit down and don't feel sleepy, then sit there. Don't open a book, just sit there. Don't turn on a radio or play recorded music. Just sit there. Look out the window if there is something good to look at out there.

Otherwise, don't look out the window. Just sit there and wait. Wait. Talk to God if you want to. Don't talk to God if you don't want to.

Talk to yourself if you want to. Don't talk to yourself if you don't want to. Either is good. Be still, be quiet, and wait. Just wait. If you feel like writing, then write whatever you want to write. Don't write if you don't feel like writing. This is a time to do whatever you feel like doing. Breathe in and out. Listen to your heart softly pounding in your chest. Listen to whatever sounds the room may make. Listen.

Wait in that room until you feel yourself from the inside out. Then, and only then, start talking to yourself or talking to God, whichever seems best at the moment. Talk about how you are feeling from the inside out. Tell God, yourself, or the room all about it. Then wait. Wait for grace from the inside out. Wait and God's own life will come to you from the inside out. It will happen if you wait. So wait. Say a prayer if you want to, and wait. Let yourself be and let God be, and quiet joy will come. It will.

This is a guaranteed way to nourish your soul. If you can.

49 ◆ *Take a Possibly Dangerous Person to Lunch*

THERE YOU ARE walking down the street, minding your own "bidness" — to quote any number of characters in stories by Flannery O'Connor. There you are walking along and a possibly dangerous person approaches you with hand outstretched. Can you spare some change? I haven't eaten all day. Maybe you're in a hurry to get to an important meeting. Probably you keep on walking, brush the beggar aside and keep on walking. This person could be dangerous.

But maybe, if you are honest with yourself, you must admit that you are not in a big hurry to get to an important meeting. You have a few minutes to spare. Make the effort. Maybe this beggar person is dangerous. It's possible. All the same, resist the urge to keep on walking, resist the urge to brush the possibly dangerous person aside and keep on walking. Resist the urge for the sake of a possibly unique and good experience that will nourish your soul, your poor neglected soul. Good.

Say this: Sorry, but I can't give you any money. But I will buy you lunch. See that fast-food-golden-fallen-arches over there? Come with me, and I will buy you a couple of cheeseburgers and something to drink of your choice. Come with me and I will buy you lunch. Come with me and I will. Say this to the possibly dangerous person. Say it and see what happens. Possibly the possibly dangerous person will follow you to the golden-fallen-arches over there. Possibly.

If this happens, and it is more than likely that it will, then go ahead and take the possibly dangerous person to lunch. Buy a couple of cheeseburgers and a drink. Give them to the possibly dangerous person. Get yourself at least a cup of coffee or a root beer and sit down with the possibly dangerous person while he or she eats the burgers from the golden-fallen-arches. If he or she wants to talk, well, listen. If he or she says nothing, ask how's it going. If the possibly dangerous person replies, well, listen. If not, then don't be pushy about it. Just sit there and sip your coffee or root beer. Just sit there.

When the possibly dangerous person finishes the cheeseburgers, say, Well, gotta go. So long and good luck. Then take your leave of the possibly dangerous person. So long and good luck. Be on your way back to work, or home, or wherever you need to go next. Be on your way, and the possibly dangerous person will be on his or her way. You have a way, and the possibly dangerous person has a way, and you both must be on your respective ways. So be on your way.

Later, tell someone else about your experience. This, too, will nourish your soul. Talking about it will nourish your soul. It will.

50 ◆ Fast for a Day

WE HAVE A THING about food. We have a thing. We eat not just for body and soul togetherness. We also eat because we have nothing else to do at the moment. We eat for recreational purposes. We eat food when what we crave most is friendship or simple companionship. We eat when we crave love. We eat when we crave God. Hard to believe, but we do.

It can nourish the soul to nourish the body, no question about it. Nourishment for soul and body often goes in through the mouth. But because we sometimes use food when what we need has nothing to do with meat and potatoes — or tofu and brown rice — it can be good for the soul to not eat. It can be good to fast. It can be good to fast for just a day or part of a day. Whatever you can get a handle on. Make up your mind to not eat between 6 a.m. and 10 p.m., for example. Or make it a full twenty-four hours. That can be good.

You might want to make your fast day a slow day, a day when not much is going on anyway. A Saturday or Sunday when you don't have to work, for example, would be a good slow day to have a fast day. You have your evening meal on Saturday knowing that you will not eat again until time for your evening meal on Sunday. This can be a good and calming thought, believe it or not.

During your fast day try to have a slow day. Do what needs to be done. Drink water and/or fruit juices. Go about your Saturday tasks, but don't overdo it. Don't try to exercise strenuously. When you feel the urge to eat, call a friend or go to visit a friend instead. When you feel the urge to eat, pray or meditate instead. If you want to be simple about it, just talk to God about it, the Divine Mystery. Here I am. Amen. Amen.

Fasting is good for the soul, but it is also good for the body. Believe it or not. When you don't eat, you give your system a rest. What a relief. Imagine if you never got to rest. Think about that for a minute. When you fast you give your stomach and the rest of your digestive tract a break. They deserve a break today. So think of a fast day as a day of rest for your body and a day of nourishment for your soul. Everybody wins.

If your stomach complains when you fast, talk to it. Have a nice little heart-to-heart with your stomach. Say: Look. It's like this. You deserve a break today. So I'm giving you a break. You are a workaholic, you know that? I fast for one day, which means you have nothing to do, and you complain. I don't believe you. Relax, willya?

51 ◆ *Stroll through a Cemetery*

DEATH AND TAXES, death and taxes, everyone agrees that nothing is certain except death and taxes. Actually, even taxes are somewhat uncertain because they can change, usually by increasing. So that leaves us with death as the only certain thing in life. Imagine that.

It can nourish your soul to stroll through a cemetery and ponder what you find there. What you find are graves, row upon row of graves. What you see is your own destiny in time and space. The day is coming when you will have no more days. But please, don't get morbid about this. That's not the idea. It's a simple fact, that's all. Your destiny, your ultimate destiny, is beyond your vision. That's all.

Your ultimate destiny lies shrouded in mystery. Still, it's not as if we have no information at all. In his book *Religion as Poetry*, Andrew M. Greeley wrote: "Religion, I assume, is the result of two incurable diseases from which humankind suffers: life, from which we die; and hope, which hints that there might be more meaning to life than a termination in death. Humankind...is the only being of which we are aware that is conscious of its own mortality and is capable of hoping that death is not the final fact in human life."

We hope. In the face of death we hope. Is this hope completely unrealistic, even naive? How, we may ask, could we propose something — in this case life beyond death — of which we have no experience? Is hope perhaps rooted in our experience, even now, of the life we will have beyond dusty death? Otherwise, what experience could our hope be rooted in? How could we dream something up that has no basis in some form of human experience?

Regardless, when you stroll through a cemetery, you see your destiny in time and space, and you may ask yourself some questions. Given that I will croak one day, how do I want to live my life? Given that I will kick the bucket, buy the farm, pass over the Great Divide, how do I want to use the time I have? Am I using it as I wish to now? What is the best way to live since I am not going to live forever?

Such questions are about ultimate values. It will nourish your soul to ponder them and be honest about your answers. To ask about death is to ask about the meaning of life — not just life in general but your life in particular. What meaning do you want your life to have? There are many directions your thoughts may take. Jean Jacques Rousseau, the eighteenth-century French philosopher, said: "When a man dies he clutches in his hands only that which he has given away in his lifetime."

You were created for a destiny beyond this life. Think about it.

52 ◆ *Smile at a Clerk in a Store Who Looks Unhappy*

IT HAPPENS all the time. You're in a store, buying a shirt, or a dress, or two tomatoes, or a package of pencils, and the clerk at the checkout stand looks less than thrilled to be doing what he or she is doing. Well, it makes sense. This can't be the most interesting job in the world. It's just a job. Just a job. But look. The minute and a half during which you stand there waiting to pay for your tomatoes or shirt is an opportunity for some human interaction. The clerk is a human being with feelings, hopes, fears, and a need for love like everyone else. This clerk may have a spouse who works hard at "just a job," too. He or she may have children. Or this clerk may have no one....

You could make eye contact and smile. Not a big deal. Or you could avoid eye contact and be merely polite. No smile. If you don't smile, if you don't make the little bit of effort required to make this a more human interaction, your soul will shrivel and be a little older when you leave the store. If you smile at the clerk, however, when you leave the store, your soul will be a little more vibrant and alive; your soul will be a bit younger than it was before.

There is so much about modern life that is depersonalized. Make a phone call to a business in the 1970s and a real live person would answer and give you the runaround. Make the same phone call today and a recorded voice gives you the runaround. If you want this department, press 1. If you want that department, press 2. If this entire experience makes you want to scream, press 3. And so forth...Even the runaround has become depersonalized.

Time was, you drove your car into what was called a "service station," and a "service station attendant" came out to pump the gasoline into your car, check the oil, and put air in your tires if needed. Today, you drive into a "convenience store," get out of your car, push a credit card into a slot on a gadget next to the gas pump, pump the gas yourself, check the oil yourself, forget about the air in your tires, get back into your car, and drive away. You have had an experience devoid of any human interaction whatsoever. Lucky you.

When an opportunity comes along to actually talk to a human being in the course of a commercial transaction, take advantage of it. Such opportunities may not exist much longer. You may go into a store to buy a couple of tomatoes one of these days and find that there is no longer any need for a clerk. You get your tomatoes, pass them over a scanner yourself, push a card into a slot to pay, and leave the store having had no human contact whatsoever. So smile while you can.

53 ◆ Daydream

DON'T JUST STAND THERE, do something. That's our cultural motto, and it's hooey. Get your nose away from the grindstone once in a while and do nothing. That makes a huge amount of sense. Stop working so hard at "having fun," too. Now and then, just sit there. Daydream. Let your mind wander wherever it will.

Some of the best ideas arrive in the middle of a daydream. If we never allow ourselves to daydream, a great many great ideas will be lost. Nourish your soul by making time to do nothing, think about nothing, accomplish nothing, and produce nothing. Let your mind wander out the door, out the window, into the clouds. See what your mind comes back with. You never know.

Some buttinski asked poet T. S. Eliot why he did not go to the movies more often. Eliot replied, "Because they interfere with my daydreams."

The crux of the matter, forsooth. You know it. Vast portions of our modern culture are dedicated to the obliteration of daydreaming. Don't kid yourself, kid. Look at television and its empty-headed progeny, all the video forms of entertainment. What do they do besides what they obviously do? They deprive us of time to daydream, that's what they do. They steal our reading time, it's true, but they also steal our daydreams and substitute cheap imitations.

A comedian said: "A thief broke into my house last night, stole everything and replaced it all with identical duplicates." Ho ho. Video forms of entertainment should do as much. But they don't. They deprive us of daydreaming time and give us in exchange the most fraudulent substitutes, somebody else's mental flapdoodle.

T. S. Eliot had no idea. All he knew were movies that you had to leave home and go to a theater to see. Now, the ideal home is an electronic entertainment center. Only superficial forms of human interaction allowed, much less daydreaming. Daydreaming looks too much like doing nothing worthwhile. Can't have that. Might have to face up to yourself and answer a few questions. Can't have that. Flip on the video entertainment equipment. Daydreaming might lead to God knows what. Erk.

Daydreaming could be dangerous, daydreaming could lead to, omygod, you know, *ideas*. Daydreaming could lead to, you know, *thoughts*. Daydreaming could be *dangerous*.

Daydream anyway. Make a choice for daydreaming because you know it will nourish your soul. It will in the most surprising ways.

54 ◆ *Bake Bread*

TALK TO ANYONE who bakes bread. They will tell you there is something spiritual about the experience from beginning to end. They will tell you. Get together the ingredients for making bread and find yourself by baking bread. It can be almost a mystical experience, and it's definitely good for your soul.

Baking bread takes time. Hours. No wonder so few people

bake bread today. No wonder big baking businesses clean up by selling us the bread they bake by the thousands upon thousands of loaves. No wonder they clean up. Mega-Bakery, Incorporated, International mixes up flour, water, yeast — plus a few other ingredients you won't find around the home (ammonium phosphate, yum!) — to make white "balloon bread" as well as other kinds of bread that also contain mysterious ingredients your grandmother never heard of. They mix it all up in bowls an elephant could take a bath in. They mix it all up and plop loaf-sized blobs of dough into mass production loaf pans, and they run those loaded pans into ovens as big as a Sherman tank. Bigger.

Baking bread takes time. Hours. Most of a day. And that's good. It means you must stay home, and that's good. You start in the morning and finish in the afternoon. Baking bread keeps you home. You mix the various ingredients, all of which have names you recognize, some of which you will find in the Bible. Yeast, for example. First the dough is sticky, then you add more flour, and more flour, and soon the dough is smooth and warm and floury.

You work at the dough, kneading it and kneading it. You work up a sweat kneading that dough with your hands. Then you put the dough back in the large bowl and cover it in a warm place, letting the yeast do its work. The dough rises while you wait. Maybe you read while the dough rises, maybe you play with your children, maybe you take a walk. When it's time, when the dough has risen, you uncover the bowl, punch down the dough, and let it rise again.

When it's time to put the dough in loaf pans, you tear off loaf-sized batches of dough and put them in the waiting loaf pans. Then you cover the pans with a towel and wait. You wait for the dough to rise again, and then into the oven go the heavy loaf pans. The aroma of baking bread is to die for. Forty-five minutes to an hour later you have bread hot from the oven. The spiritual process of baking bread is complete. Except for one thing.

Now you eat the hot bread with butter on it. Real butter. Damn the calories and the cholesterol and full speed ahead. It nourishes your soul.

55 ◆ *Read the Bible*

WE LIVE in our culture like a fish swims in water. It's not something you can walk away from; you can't simply decide one day to stop being a fish and become, instead, a bird. No gonna happen. We are creatures of the Western world, and our culture is deeply rooted in the traditions and thought patterns of Christianity and Judaism.

More precisely, people who are born in and bred on Western culture are far more likely to find meaning and light in the sacred writings called the Bible — the Hebrew and Christian Scriptures — than in the Upanishads, the Qur'an, or other sacred writings from other cultures. Understanding even such things as the literature and poetry of the United States and England requires familiarity with the Bible. You'll get no place with William Blake or William Faulkner, not to mention Flannery O'Connor, unless you have a good grasp of the contents and meaning of the Bible.

To nourish your soul, read the Bible. If you know it from your childhood only, a new world is in store for you as an adult. Perhaps you know the Bible only as literature. Know that its pages carry the sacred for those who read it not with the intellect only but with the soul. At their deepest levels, the so-called "Old" and "New" Testaments connect with your soul and nourish it with the life of the Divine Mystery itself. These sacred writings bear a God who is not just an impersonal Deity but a compassionate, forgiving, guiding Love who is interested in you as a unique and irreplaceable individual whose existence transcends space and time.

Pick up a good translation of the Bible. (The New Revised Standard Version is perhaps the best there is.) Read a good book on reading the Bible with intelligence, and ponder the Hebrew Scriptures:

> So now, O Israel, what does the LORD your God require of you? Only to fear the LORD your God, to walk in all his ways, to love him, to serve the LORD your God with all your heart and with all your soul, and to keep the commandments of the LORD your God and his decrees that I am commanding you today, for your own well-being. (Deut. 10:12–13)

"For your own well-being." Imagine that. Let the words sink into your soul; don't let them simply float on the surface of your intellect. Don't analyze; soak up. Let the words live in your heart and they will nourish your soul.

Now read from the Christian Scriptures:

> Whoever says, "I am in the light," while hating a brother or sister, is still in the darkness. Whoever loves a brother or sister lives in the light, and in such a person there is no cause for stumbling. (1 John 2:9–10)

Once again, let the words sink into your soul. Don't remain an objective, detached observer. Let the sacred words nourish your soul.

56 ◆ *Read the Sacred Writings of Other Cultures*

WHILE the Hebrew and Christian Scriptures offer the sacred writings that denizens of Western cultures find it most natural to connect with, don't underestimate the light to be found in the sacred writings of other cultures, as well. The Bible is "ours," but countless millions find divine light in other writings, and we too may find wisdom there. Reading the sacred writings of other cultures can be a mind- and soul-expanding experience.

Pick up a copy of the Qur'an. Have you ever looked at it before? What are your presuppositions and prejudices about Islam? Read the words with your mind, of course, but try to let the words hit you on a deeper level as well.

> Jews say: "Christians have no point to make"; while Christians say: "The Jews have no point to make." They (all) quote from the [same] Book. Likewise those who do not know anything make a statement similar to theirs. God will judge between them on Resurrection Day concerning how they have been differing. ("The Cow," I, 2:113; xiv)

To open the pages of another culture's sacred writings is to step into another world, another way of thinking, something completely foreign. At the same time, don't overlook our common humanity. If religion or spirituality do not lead us to universal compassion, what good are they?

Meditate upon some words from the *Bhagavad Gita,* sacred writings from the Hindu religion and culture of India that celebrate themes not unlike those found in the writings of many

Western Christian mystics. These themes clash with the materialism and enthusiasm for "results" which Western cultures cherish.

> Set thy heart upon thy work, but never on its reward. Work not for a reward; but never cease to do thy work.
>
> Do thy work in the peace of Yoga and, free from selfish desires, be not moved in success or in failure. Yoga is evenness of mind — a peace that is ever the same. (2:47–48)

Buddhism has its sacred writings, as well, by various authors at various times and places. Buddhism is not a "religion of the Book" in the same sense as Judaism, Christianity, and Islam. But its sacred writings carry no less wisdom if we refuse to allow apparent contradictions to block our sensitivity to the spiritual light.

> As a mother, who at the risk of her life watches over her only child, so let everyone cultivate a boundless friendly mind toward all beings. And let him cultivate goodwill toward all the world, a boundless friendly mind, above, below and across, unobstructed, without hatred, without enmity, standing, walking, sitting or lying — as long as he is awake, let him devote himself to this mind. (*Mettasutta*)

Let the light of sacred writings fall upon your open mind and heart. Welcome truth whatever its source. Visit other traditions, and then carry the wisdom you find back to your own tradition. This will nourish your soul.

57 ◆ *Help Out in a Soup Kitchen or Homeless Shelter*

CHANCES ARE if you're reading this book you are not homeless and you take none of your meals in a soup kitchen. We live in astonishing times, for countless people are homeless and countless people turn to soup kitchens and hot meal programs of various kinds for the nourishment they need to keep body and soul together. To be out of touch with these people, our fellow human beings, is to be out of touch with a big part of the culture and society we inhabit.

Nourish your soul. Help out in a soup kitchen or shelter for homeless people. Overcome your anxiety, your fear even, and volunteer. Call or stop by. Talk with whoever you need to talk with about volunteering. Take the first step, then another step, then another, until you are in the door and doing something, anything, to help out. It's not difficult. The tough part is getting past your own anxieties and ignorance. These are not dangerous people. They're just people. Like you. Just like you. So don't be afraid.

Someone on the staff at the soup kitchen or homeless shelter will take you under his or her wing and guide you along. You will get to know people you would never get to know otherwise or anywise. The people on the regular staff will impress and irritate you. Hey, they're only human. Like you. The people who come for food and/or shelter will touch your heart and get on your nerves. Hey, they're only human. Like you. If you withhold judgment—condemn no one and put no one on a pedestal, even in the silence of your heart—you will gain wisdom and insight you never thought to possess. You will.

Soup kitchens, inner-city hot meal programs, and shelters for homeless people are not charity. They are simple justice. When there is plenty for everyone but some don't have enough, something is seriously wrong. It's easy to wag your finger at people who are hungry or homeless and accuse them of laziness or lack of personal resourcefulness. It's easy. Get to know a few people who are hungry or homeless and you find that your easy assumptions were foolish assumptions. The reality of hunger and homelessness has nothing to do with our preconceived notions. Nothing at all. To open yourself to reality nourishes your soul, even when the reality is no fun to look at.

When you help out at the soup kitchen or shelter for homeless people, don't remain on the sidelines very long. Get involved. Get to know the people you're working with. Get to know the people you are there to serve. Get to know them all as human beings, not as "a problem" or as statistics. Get to know them up-close. It will nourish your soul.

58 ◆ *Write an Essay Giving Your Opinion*

THINKING AND WRITING go together. Sometimes you may not know what you think until you write. You like something going on in society at large? Sit down and write a short essay explaining what you like and why. You disagree with something? Write an essay about it. Putting words on paper helps you to clarify your own thoughts and get them in order. It's not unusual for newspapers to publish well-written opinion pieces, so once you have yours in order send it off. Even if it doesn't appear in print, it will be time well spent.

Don't think that an essay must focus on politics. Sometimes the most personal experiences have the widest interest. What strikes you as important because it affects your children or your family will, most likely, be of equal interest to countless other families or parents. Most significant, however, is the impact writing will have on your own soul. To write is to discover something new about yourself, about who you are and your place in the world.

Sometimes when people decide to write they presume that writing is a formal activity. Must have all this equipment, computers, and so forth. Such an attitude may lead to premature discouragement. In one of his Winnie the Pooh stories, A. A. Milne has the grumpy donkey Eeyore say: "This writing business, pencils and what-not. Overrated if you ask me."

Writing is not primarily a technical activity; it's a spiritual one. All you need is a comfortable setting, paper, and a pen or pencil. Take a lesson from Mark Twain, who was fond of writing in bed, regardless of the time of day. One time his wife came in to announce that a reporter was at the door to interview him for a newspaper. When Twain showed no sign of getting up, she said, "Don't you think it will be a little embarrassing for him to find you in bed?"

"Why, if you think so, Livy," Twain replied, "we could have the other bed made up for him."

You don't write merely to express your thoughts. More to the point, you write to express your *self,* your unique person and presence in the world. In order to do this, you must believe that you have a self worth giving away. Believe this. You are a completely unique person with unique contributions to make, and if you don't make them they will be lost to the world for all time. Don't laugh about this. The temptation to hunker down and conform, or give in to the mass mind, is powerful. Instead, think for yourself and express your unique thoughts when you write.

Write to express yourself, no matter what the topic, and then try to get your thoughts into print. This is a process that will nourish your soul.

59 ◆ *Give God a Piece of Your Mind*

YOU HAVE PROBABLY seen either a stage production or the movie version of *Fiddler on the Roof.* Recall the scene where Tevye, the poor Jewish milkman, complains to God: "Would it spoil some vast eternal plan / If I were a wealthy man?"

Tevye is on intimate terms with God. He has great respect for his Creator, but he feels free to gripe and complain, as well, and this is a soul-nourishing activity. You may have the inclination, when something bad happens, to be merely submissive, to say to God, "Thy will be done," and let it go at that. But maybe that's not the healthiest attitude, spiritually speaking. Maybe it's better to be completely honest with God. Perhaps the Great Cosmic Wherewithal can take whatever you can dish out.

The Book of Psalms, in the Hebrew Scriptures/Old Testament, is loaded with honest human emotions directed at God, everything from anger and complaint to thanksgiving and praise. The Psalms run the gamut of human emotions.

"Why, O LORD, do you stand far off? Why do you hide yourself in times of trouble?" (10:1). Words such as these are prayer every bit as much as those that sound more reverent or pious. In the same way, you can be honest with God by questioning God or getting angry with God. To do this is to nourish your soul in deep and satisfying ways. God can take it.

Are you angry about something going on in your life or in the world? Are you feeling angry with God because of this? Then raise hell with God. Tell God how you feel about it. You may be surprised at the results of such a prayer. And it *is* prayer. You may receive a "message" in return that you would never expect.

An example: a young woman was expecting her first baby, and she miscarried. She and her husband were sad, of course. But before long the young woman realized that she was not just sad but angry. She took a walk in a deserted suburban park, and as she walked she cried and told the Creator of the universe how angry she was. "I'm angry at you, God," she said. "Why did you let this happen? Why? Why?"

Suddenly, the young woman "heard" in her heart a voice saying, "I want this baby to be with me now. That's all you need to know."

The young woman was filled with peace; she was reconciled to what had happened, but this might never have happened had she not allowed herself to be angry with God, had she not told God how she felt. Being honest with God allowed her to work through this painful experience and come out healthy and at peace on the other side.

So be honest about your feelings with God.

60 ◆ *Take Care of Yourself*

THERE IS AN ATTITUDE floating around in our culture according to which it is selfish to ever focus on yourself. Nothing could be further from the truth. You need to spend time on yourself regularly, "recharging your batteries," if you expect to have the resources to care for others. A life centered on other people is the only happy life, but you need time to "refuel" in order to live such a life.

Parents are a perfect example. Raising children is a tremendously rewarding activity, but it's also a hugely challenging and draining activity. You need regular times to get away from your children. You need time with your spouse and/or time simply to be alone, to relax, to have some recreational time to yourself. The demands of children are constant, so you need to be disciplined enough to say, "Enough!"

Parents are not the only ones who need time for themselves.

The inclination can be powerful to never get away from your work. For some people work is life and life is work. They forget that no matter how rewarding one's work may be, still, we should work to live, not live to work. You need time away, time to relax, time to simply be. This is true for any kind of work but especially true for work that is people-oriented.

If you are in a people-helping profession, you need to stop helping people and spend time on yourself. You can't help them if you don't help yourself. Get away. Relax. Stay on top of life; don't let life get on top of you. You can't give to others if you have nothing to give.

This is no esoteric matter. Even the work that you do depends on taking care of yourself. Louis Brandeis, a famous early twentieth-century justice of the Supreme Court, was once criticized for taking time off just before the start of an important trial. "I need the rest," Brandeis explained. "I find that I can do a year's work in eleven months, but I can't do it in twelve."

Motive is the crux of the matter. Taking time for yourself can and should be an entirely unselfish commitment. You take time away from your family for the sake of your family. You take time away from your spouse for the sake of your marriage. You take time to read a book so you'll be a more interesting person for others and so you'll have a new idea to share with others. You take time to attend a concert so you'll be a happier person for others to be around.

Sometimes people accuse those who meditate of "navel gazing." Nonsense. You meditate in order to be more at peace and have more personal depth to share with others.

61 ◆ *Commune with Nature*

WE ARE first of all a part of nature. We belong here on the earth with the plants and animals, breathing the air, drinking the water. We belong here. So easy to forget this. We build cities of concrete, asphalt, steel, plastic, and glass. We surround ourselves with an artificial environment, cutting ourselves off from the rhythms of nature. Artificial this, imitation that.

We don't even use our bodies the way they are designed to be used. Instead of walking we ride in machines with wheels from here to there and back again. Our legs don't get the use they should. Instead of climbing stairs we ride elevators and escalators. We drag our bodies around, almost, making much less use of our muscles than our grandparents and great-grandparents did.

Out of touch with nature. Artificial light is a biggie. We hardly know what darkness is anymore. At night we simply switch from natural light to artificial light. So we don't have the deep appreciation for light that people had not so long ago. We don't know what the stars look like at night because the artificial light makes it difficult to see the stars.

Even our food is something less than natural. So much of what we eat is heavily processed and "seasoned" with chemical additives. Even the vegetables we buy in a supermarket are processed and chemically treated — chemical fertilizers, chemical sprays to kill insects. What's up, Doc? A carrot doesn't taste much like a carrot. You discover this if you compare the flavor of the average supermarket carrot with a carrot you grow yourself or if you buy an organically grown carrot.

We are first of all a part of nature, but we're alienated from nature in many ways by our culture. If you make the extra effort to be more in touch with nature, it will nourish your soul.

We are alienated from nature, but we don't forget our need to be in touch with the natural world. We build parks even in our biggest cities, and weekends and holidays the parks fill with people to overcrowding. We need to be with the trees, flowers, and water in the ponds. In Tokyo, a few ducks arrive each year to stay in an cement pool in the middle of the city, and countless people stand around watching the mother duck and her growing ducklings. It's a natural event, and Tokyo is not long on nature. We need to be in touch with our natural environment, with animals and plants.

You need to sit on a rock on the edge of a lake and simply look at the lake. You need to walk through a forest and sleep under the stars without the benefit of artificial light. You need to do these things. It's absolutely necessary to nourish your soul.

62 ◆ Become a Vegetarian...
at Least Temporarily

TIME WAS people who did not eat meat were a rare breed. Seventh-day Adventists. Trappist monks. The odd Bohemian or the occasional nut case. Real people ate meat, by God.

Times have changed, the culture has shifted, there is a lot we know about what's good for human beings to eat and what isn't. We have big problems with cholesterol and fat, and eating a lot of red meat is no help. We also know that you must feed cattle many pounds of grain protein to get a single pound of meat protein, grain that could be used to feed people who are hungry. All kinds of social, political, and philosophical issues converge on the issue of nutrition.

A vegetarian diet has much in its favor. You won't die if you don't eat meat. In fact, you will probably be healthier if you don't eat meat. At the very least give it a try on a temporary basis and see how it goes. Choose an appropriate time. Christians may find Lent a good time for such an experiment. But any time is a good time. Try a vegetarian diet for a week or two. It can nourish your soul if for no other reason than you are taking charge of your life, stepping out of something taken for granted in the great cultural loop.

Try a vegetarian diet, but don't run off half-cocked. This is not a haphazard experiment. Get some good resources, a couple of vegetarian cook books for starters. Plan in advance how you will deal with situations where everyone else eats meat — in a restaurant, for example. What will you say when the others in your group kid you about not eating meat? How will you stay with your experiment without getting defensive or self-righteous about it?

To become a vegetarian, even if only temporarily, will nourish your soul because it requires you to take charge of your life instead of going along with what comes most easily. To try a vegetarian diet requires you to become more aware of yourself and your world. It means facing up to who controls your life, cultural pressures or you? Do you always do what comes most easily or are you willing to swim upstream for the sake of what you may learn from the experience about yourself and the world?

Igor Stravinsky, the great Russian-born composer, during a vegetarian phase had dinner with fellow composer Nicholas Nabokov. Nabokov left some of his cutlet, and Stravinsky asked if he might finish it. Swallowing the bite of meat with a dollop of sour cream, he said, "I want to astonish the raw potato in my stomach."

Be a vegetarian, temporarily or permanently, but don't take yourself too seriously. Otherwise it won't nourish your soul.

63 ◆ *Have Faith and Pray When You Are Ill*

P EOPLE have the strangest notions, sometimes, when it comes to faith. Some people think faith means you must never think critically or ask questions or have doubts. Some people think faith means accepting the reality of a Supreme Being of which you have no experience and no proof. In fact, faith means two things. It means believing that our tendency to hope is not founded on an illusion. It also means that we continue to be connected to the unseen but real and loving source of our existence.

One of the most remarkable developments in our understanding of faith since the early 1980s comes from the world of medicine and scientific research. A significant number of physicians and scientists find strong evidence for a faith-body connection that has a healing effect. "Someday, instead of 'Take two aspirins and call me in the morning,' we may be saying 'Take two prayers,'" said Dr. David Larson, a psychiatrist and director of the National Institute of Healthcare Research in Rockville, Maryland. "God is good for you," Dr. Larson told James D. Davis of the *Fort Lauderdale Sun-Sentinel.*

"The evidence is overwhelming that religion, spirituality, faith — however you name it — is a protective factor against illness," said Jeff Levin, an epidemiologist at Eastern Virginia Medical School in Norfolk, Virginia.

Larry Dossey, M.D., offers even more convincing information in his book *Healing Words: The Power of Prayer and the Practice of Medicine.* "Over time," Dossey wrote, "I decided that *not* to employ prayer with my patients was the equivalent of deliberately withholding a potent drug or surgical procedure.... I simply could not ignore the evidence for prayer's effectiveness without feeling like a traitor to the scientific tradition."

Faith, at its most fundamental level, is a relationship between the human person and the Divine Mystery. The relationship that exists between you and God, that's faith. When you are healthy you should take that relationship into account and cultivate it. When you are ill you should do the same. Healthy or sick, nourish your soul by cultivating your relationship with God. Do this by being a prayerful person at all times and in all places, for God is closer to you than you are to yourself at all times and in all places.

When you are ill, follow the doctor's directions and ask God to be present to you in your illness, not in spite of it. Pray that God's will may be done. Then relax and allow yourself to fall into what an earlier generation called "the Everlasting Arms." Fall, fall, fall into God's infinite, unconditional, absolutely trustworthy love. Abandon yourself completely.

64 ◆ *Stop Trying to Fix Yourself*

IN HIS MARVELOUS BOOK *Simply Sane*, Gerald May, M.D., observes that by the time most of us reach age twenty-one we have gone crazy a few times and sane a few times. Many people decide that crazy is preferable to sane, so they spend much effort trying to "make some thing of themselves."

They decide that seeking financial security, status, and respect are the way to find meaning in life. Others dedicate themselves to raising healthy, well-adjusted children, and they do that. More or less. Others choose such goals and fail. They flunk out of school, lose the "good job," or botch what could have been a good marriage.

Regardless of whether we "succeed" or "fail" at the goals we set for ourselves, it's not unusual to reach a certain point in life and ask if it has all been worth the effort. People seek a new direction. They take a course, join a group, dedicate themselves to a cause, or go into psychotherapy. The goal in each case is to "fix" oneself, manipulate one's self. Such folks forget that the voice of sanity has another message. Sanity says, "Allow yourself to accept yourself as you are and simply be who you are. Allow yourself to stop trying to fix yourself."

Don't just do something. Stand there. This is the voice of sanity. Religion and living are the same. Accept. Live. Immerse yourself in the process of living. You are, that's all that matters. Go about your life, your daily tasks, your responsibilities, just being. Allow yourself to stop trying to live and just live.

If you are a parent, allow yourself to abandon the notion that you have complete control over your children. Allow yourself to do your best as a parent, do what you think is right. Then allow yourself to watch your children grow. Allow yourself to just watch because in the long run that's all you can do anyway.

Allow yourself to have faith or give up, whichever you feel most like doing. Six of one, half-dozen of the other. "Hope is like despair, it won't get you anywhere," wrote singer/song writer John Stewart. Allow yourself to leap into faith that you are loved with an infinite love and need do nothing. Or allow yourself to despair of ever being able to "get your act together" and discover that this, too, is a pathway to equanimity and acceptance. Allow yourself to give up or have faith; they both will lead you to being yourself and being.

Allow yourself to give up reading self-help books and pop psychology. Allow yourself to give up searching for your inner child. Allow yourself to be yourself instead of trying to fix yourself.

65 ◆ *Find a Hero*

WE LIVE in an era of disillusionment and cynicism. We find it difficult to believe that anyone could be a hero. If someone looks heroic, it probably means he or she has a good publicist. If someone looks heroic, you are foolish to take it seriously because undoubtedly the public image is out of synch with the real person. He or she couldn't be a hero because being human is incompatible with true heroism.

Young people, especially, have trouble identifying heroes. Sports celebrities and rock music stars get major media attention, but as heroes they don't hold up well, what with widespread substance abuse problems, the occasional suicide, and so forth. If young people admire sports and rock music stars often it's because they, too, would like to be rich and famous. Wealth and lifestyles of conspicuous consumption hardly reflect courage and strength, however.

The trouble is not with the availability of true heroes; the trouble is with our understanding of heroism. A hero is not a person who has no faults, who never makes a mistake, or never acts out of selfishness or narrow-mindedness. Rather, a hero is someone who acts with courage and strength even though his or her life may also reveal actions that fail to measure up to a heroic standard. A hero is strong and courageous even though his or her life may reveal instances of weakness and cowardice, as well. When the cards are on the table, a true hero is strong and courageous regardless of how he or she acted before.

The twentieth century offers more than a few heroes if we care to look for them, although in most cases they had their dark sides as well. Eleanor Roosevelt, Martin Luther King, Jr., Jacqueline Kennedy Onassis, Robert Kennedy, Golda Meir, John F. Kennedy, Dorothy Day, and Raoul Wallenberg come to mind.

A hero need not be a famous person, of course. In fact, most of the people who act with heroic strength and courage never become famous. All you need do is think about your own life and the people you have known. Perhaps your grandparents or parents are your heroes. Maybe you had a friend along the way who serves as your hero. The important thing is to identify a strong and courageous person, famous or obscure, whom you would like to identify with, look up to, admire and imitate.

Nourish your soul by finding a hero. Read about him or her. Get a picture of your hero and put it in a place where you'll see it every day. Write down a quotation from your hero and memorize it. You need a hero because we all need to see strength, courage, goodness, and virtue embodied in the life of a real person. We need someone to look up to.

I T'S FAIRLY EASY to be generous once, spontaneously. Someone comes to the door collecting money to help find lost children or finance research on Alzheimer's disease. You give five bucks. Someone takes up a collection at the office to help a fellow employee whose child is seriously ill. You kick in ten bucks. Both of these actions are good. They nourish the soul. But it can nourish your soul on a long-term, perhaps deeper, basis to commit yourself to being generous over the long haul.

Commit yourself to being generous even when you may not feel generous or when you may not feel like you can afford to be generous. Write a letter to a favorite charity promising to give a certain amount of money each month for twelve consecutive months. Promise to be generous even if you don't know whether you will have the money to be generous with a few months from now. Promise to give money to help those less fortunate than yourself even if you have no job security to speak of.

Why does giving away money nourish one's soul? It's not so much the money that matters as our feelings and attitudes toward money. We tend to think of money as the ultimate form of security. If you have lots of money you are secure, and the more money you have the more secure you are. The more money you have the happier you will be.

It nourishes the soul to give away money because we believe that money is the ultimate source of happiness and security. Money is necessary, it's true. We need money to pay our way in the world, and lack of money can be a terrific evil. There is nothing good about economic poverty. The trouble is that most of us think we need far more money than we actually need. So it nourishes the soul to give some away regularly.

The point is to free yourself from slavery to financial anxieties. When you give away some money you free yourself a little bit more from being controlled by money and the desire for money. If you don't have much money, don't give away much money. If you have more than enough money, give away more than you are comfortable giving away. When you act in this way you nourish your soul because you free your soul.

Here is a famous quotation: "Money is the root of all evil."

This is a misquote. Here are the actual words from the Christian Scriptures: "For the love of money is a root of all kinds of evil" (1 Tim. 6:10).

It's not money that is the root of all evil; it's the *love* of money that is the problem. "Keep your lives free from the love of money, and be content with what you have; for [God] has said, 'I will never leave you or forsake you'" (Heb. 13:5).

67 ◆ *Make a Promise and Keep It No Matter What*

ONE OF THE MOST BASIC SIGNS of personal maturity is the capacity to do what you say you are going to do. You say to someone, "I'll meet you on Thursday at 7 p.m." A mature adult will be there at 7 p.m. on Thursday come hell or high water. Either that or telephone ahead of time: "Sorry, I can't make it because of hell and high water. How about if we reschedule for next week?" If you promise to be there and simply do not show up, the person you were supposed to meet will begin to think that you are an unreliable person whose word is not to be trusted.

François Edouard Joachim Coppée was a late nineteenth-century French poet who became a member of the French Academy in 1884. The wife of a not too distinguished writer once asked Coppée to support her husband's candidacy for a place in the Academy, which would be a great honor and would further her husband's career. "I beg you, vote for my husband," she pleaded. "He'll die if he's not elected."

François Coppée agreed, but his vote failed to get the woman's husband into the French Academy. A few months later another seat became vacant and the woman returned begging Coppée to vote for her husband once again. "Ah, no," replied Coppée. "I kept my promise but he did not keep his. I consider myself free of any obligation."

This was a case, humorous of course, where one person — the poet Coppée — took his promise seriously but was unwilling to make another promise he was not willing to keep. He used the woman's exaggeration about her husband's certain death to put a light spin on the situation rather than say he would do something he could not. Coppée could have said that he would vote again for the woman's husband and then not have voted for him. Instead, he told the truth.

How seriously do we take the making of promises and commitments? How seriously do we take it when we make a vow to stay married to the same person "as long as we both shall live"? If surveys and statistics reveal anything, they suggest that many people simply do not take such commitments seriously. So far has our culture taken this that some people don't bother with the vow in the first place. Many others think to themselves, "Well, I would like this to last as long as we both shall live, but if it doesn't, that's the way the cookie crumbles. C'est la vie."

This leaves the back door open for a convenient escape, as it were. If this gets to be too much work, I can skip out. There are circumstances which make it wise to end a marriage, of course. But in many cases divorce is more of a convenience than anything else, an easy out in a culture averse to growing up.

68 ◆ Enjoy Yourself in a Way That Costs No Money

THOMAS MERTON, the famous mid-twentieth-century Trappist monk, author, and poet, once remarked that you should enjoy watching the rain fall before someone figures out a way to charge you for it. He wasn't far from the truth, either. Think of your favorite ways to relax and enjoy life. How many of them require you to buy something or pay someone?

Nourish your soul. Enjoy yourself in a way that requires you to spend no money at all. In a book called *Following Christ in a Consumer Society*, John Francis Kavanaugh wrote:

> Let us suppose you are a married person with children. If you are relatively happy with your life, if you enjoy spending time with your children, playing with them and talking with them; if you like nature, if you enjoy sitting in your yard or on your front steps, if your sexual life is relatively happy, if you have a peaceful sense of who you are and are stabilized in your relationships, if you like to pray in solitude, if you just like talking to people, visiting them, spending time in conversation with

them, if you enjoy living simply, if you sense no need to compete with your friends or neighbors — *what good are you economically* in terms of our system? You haven't spent a nickel yet.

That's the idea. Nourish your soul in a way that relies on human relationships rather than technology or expensive equipment. Find a way to enjoy yourself with others that doesn't cost a cent or at least doesn't require you to buy anything you don't already have. Here are some ideas:

- Read a book by your favorite poet.
- Go for a walk with a family member or friend.
- Play a board game or card game with a neighbor.
- Invite some friends over to talk about soul nourishing.
- Make love with your spouse *before* bedtime when you're too tired.
- Watch the rain fall.
- Watch the snow fall.
- Lie on your back outside on a clear night and look at the stars.
- Get recordings of some old radio programs from the public library and listen to them with your family or with some friends.
- Write a poem about falling in love.
- Read aloud to your children, no matter how old they are.

Leisure time should be a time to simply be with no need to participate in the economy by spending money. Shopping as a form of recreation is phony. It's exhausting and, in the long run, unsatisfying. Most of the time all shopping does is cultivate acquisitiveness and temporarily satiate the endless thirst for more and more "stuff."

Nourish your soul by doing something that requires you to stay home, go no place, and spend no money.

69 ◆ *Go on a Silent Retreat*

THE WILDEST VARIETY of activities go by the name "retreat," and many of them amount to worthwhile activities. There are retreats for groups of fellow employees, Twelve Step retreats, retreats for every self-help group you can imagine, literary retreats, musical retreats, retreats for married couples and engaged couples, and retreats for divorced people and single parents.

There is much to be said for a traditional silent retreat, however. There is much to be said for spending a few days in silence with nobody to talk to except yourself and the Great Cosmic Wherewithal. There is much to be said for having nothing in particular to do, no plans, no goals to meet, no deadlines, the simplest of structure for your day. There is something to be said for sitting still.

No matter where you live there is probably a retreat facility within driving distance. Most retreat facilities are sponsored by religious institutions. Some are monasteries. Almost always, however, the people who operate these facilities don't give a tinker's damn about your religious inclinations or loyalties, if any. You make a reservation, you arrive, you show up for meals; other than that you're on your own. If you want someone to talk with — a spiritual guide or whatever — you will be provided with one. You want to be left alone, you'll be left alone. You want to attend talks on various topics, you attend the talks. You don't want to attend the talks, you don't attend.

A silent retreat is a time to listen mostly to yourself, to get back in touch with what's most important to you. A silent retreat is a time to listen mostly to the Divine Mystery speaking to you in your own life and experience. Frederick Buechner put it this way: "Listen to your life. See it for the fathomless mystery that it is. In the boredom and pain of it no less than in the excitement and gladness: touch, taste, smell your way to the holy and hidden heart of it because in the last analysis all moments are key moments and life itself is grace."

Getting back in touch with the truth that your life itself is grace, that's what a silent retreat is for. It's also time to remember that you are free, you are not a mere consumer, you do not exist to respond to the whims of the fashion industry, or the entertainment industry, or any other industry. You are free to live your life for what matters most, your relationships with other people and your loving intimacy with God. You are free to live a life centered on joy, you are free to ignore the pressures the dominant culture puts on everyone to be anxious and act out of fear. A silent retreat is a time to remember that you are free.

70 ◆ *Tell Someone You Love, "I Love You"*

L OVE MEANS knowing you can rely on the other person to be there. Love means knowing you can trust the other person. Love means knowing that the other person will not abandon you. All this adds up to one of life's most worthwhile experiences, the feeling of being loved by another.

This experience of love has its dark side, however. When you know you can rely on the other person to be there you tend to slip, without even thinking about it, into a trap. The trap is called taking for granted the one who loves you, and nobody likes to feel taken for granted. Nobody, regardless of how deeply that person loves you. Nobody, nowhere, no how, likes to feel taken for granted.

We are fearfully fragile beings, we humans. We need to feel loved, especially by the ones who are most important to us, the ones we make promises and commitments to. So easily we begin to feel taken for granted, so easily we begin to feel unloved. So fearfully fragile we are that we need to hear that we are loved, we need to hear from the people we love that they love us. We need to *feel* loved or the love of the other begins to seem unreal, a fiction, something rumored to have happened in the past but unconnected to the present.

There is a wonderful scene in the musical *Fiddler on the Roof.* Tevye asks Golda, his wife of twenty-five years, "Do you love me?" She responds with a list of all the things she has done for him for the last quarter century: washed his clothes, cooked his meals, cleaned his house, given him children, milked the cow. "After twenty-five years why talk about love right now?" Golda sings.

Tevye persists: "Do you love me?" Still Golda equivocates: "I'm your wife." Tevye asks again, "Do you love me?" Golda comes up with another list. For twenty-five years she has "lived with him, fought with him, starved with him; twenty-five years my bed is his. If that's not love what is?"

Overjoyed, Tevye sings: "Then you love me!" Golda: "I suppose I do." Tevye: "And I suppose I love you, too." Together they sing: "It doesn't change a thing, but even so. After twenty-five years it's nice to know."

We show our love for those we love in countless ways every day and over the years. But we don't want to feel taken for granted. We want to hear that we are loved. We want to hear, "I love you." We want to receive flowers. We want to get little signs and gestures that say, "I do not take you for granted."

Giving those signs and gestures will nourish your soul.

71 ◆ *Do Something You've Never Done Before*

WE ARE CREATURES of habit, preferring the familiar to the strange or new. Given a choice between the path not taken and the well-beaten path we'll take the latter every time, thank you. Give us a choice between security and opportunity and we are most likely to choose security. We may complain about having a boring life, but we would rather have boredom than a genuine adventure.

In one of his old stand-up routines comic Bill Cosby remarked that when his daughters were babies the one thing he would not do was change diapers. "Do not like surprises," he quipped. How like us all. We have no great affection for the unexpected. Yet one of the best ways to nourish your soul is to take a chance and do something you have never done before. For almost everyone it is not difficult to think of things you have never done before.

Think about it. Think. This may take the form of a risk-taking adventure. Parachute out of an airplane. Take a ride in a hot air balloon. Join a group for rafting down huge, boiling rapids on a river in Idaho or Colorado. Learn to ride a skate board or how to use in-line skates. Go rock climbing or mountain climbing. Ride a bicycle for a very long distance, say a ride of a week or two.

All such activities are exciting, even terrifying, because they are small encounters with your fear of the unknown and unexpected. You never know what might happen. The thing is that most of the time they lead you to no harm. You jump out of the airplane and your parachute opens drifting you lightly to the ground. Your risk-taking adventure becomes a small experience of the ultimate risk, namely, death. Just as your parachute opened when you jumped out of the airplane, you will find yourself safe on the other side of death.

Another approach is to learn a skill you never tried before. Learn to play the banjo or the saxophone. Learn welding or auto mechanics. Learn to change the oil in your car. Take lessons in basket weaving or glass blowing, how to use a computer or Chinese cookery. To pick up a new skill is to stretch yourself, expand your soul, open yourself to new dimensions of life.

The key element is risk. Choose a new activity that carries some risk for you. Stick your neck out. Step outside the safe, predictable boundaries of your present life into the realm of the uncertain. Go back to school no matter what your age. Begin work on a college degree or graduate degree no matter what your age. Set some new goals for yourself. Push back your outer limits.

72 ◆ *Do Somebody Else's Chores*

WE LIVE in an age of egalitarianism. Everybody should have his or her own household chores to do, regardless of age, sex, race, or religion. If you live here you do your part, you carry your share of the load. No freeloading and no free lunch. This is a fine approach, good old democracy at work right here on the old homestead.

For all its value, however, sometimes this approach to household chores can lead to nit-picking and legalism. That's your job, not mine. I did my job. Egalitarianism in household responsibilities may lend itself to a "this far and no farther" approach to basic human relationships. I do what I'm supposed to do and that's all I am going to do. So there.

Yes, it's your job to take out the trash, and it's my job to vacuum the carpets, and it's his job to clean the upstairs bathroom. All the same...once in a while it's good for the soul to pitch in and do someone else's chore. Your spouse needs to be out of town this weekend on business, so what the heck. Go ahead and do her job for her. Your daughter has an early soccer game this Saturday, so clean the bathroom for her as a surprise.

The same principle applies on the job. Your responsibilities are clearly outlined in your job description, yes. It's not your job to convey the bratz wonkers to the overhead whistle loopers, especially not on Wednesdays. But you are all caught up on your work and your co-worker is behind on getting those bratz wonkers to the overhead whistle loopers. So lend a hand. It's not your job, but lend a hand.

There are all kinds of ways you can nourish your soul by doing what you have no responsibility for doing. You're walking through the park or down the sidewalk in your neighborhood. Some old newspapers or candy wrappers are on the ground. Either the wind blew them out of a trash receptacle or a thoughtless person simply threw them on the ground. Either way, it's not your responsibility to clean up litter. Granted. But it will do your soul good to pick up those old newspapers or candy wrappers and get them into the nearest trash can. It's not your job, but do it anyway.

Your elderly neighbor needs to spend a couple of weeks in the hospital. You have no obligation to mow her lawn and keep it watered. Do it all the same.

A car is stopped along the side of the road with an obviously flat tire. The teenage driver doesn't seem to know what to do about it. In a flash you either decide to stop and help or keep on driving. You have no obligation to stop, but you will feel good about it if you do. So stop. Help the kid change the tire. It will nourish your soul.

73 ◆ *Take a Nursing Home Resident Out to Lunch*

WE FIND IT so easy to forget about old people, particularly if they are very old and feeble. The one thing old age seems to qualify people for in our society is being ignored. Out of sight out of mind.

Casey Stengel was the wily and witty manager of the champion New York Yankees for thirteen years (1949–62) and the New York Mets for three years (1962–65). Explaining a fine point of baseball to young baseball star Mickey Mantle, the seventy-year-old Stengel used an incident from his own playing days to illustrate his point. "You played?" Mantle asked. "Sure I played," said Stengel. "Did you think I was born at the age of seventy sitting in a dugout trying to manage guys like you?"

We forget that old people had a life before we existed. We forget that they were children, adolescents, young adults, and people with families of their own, with work they did every day for many years. We forget that most of what we feel and think they felt and thought a long time ago. We find it difficult to think of old people as people.

John Quincy Adams (1767–1848), sixth president of the United States, suffered a stroke, and his health was clearly failing. Daniel Webster described his last meeting with Adams: "Someone, a friend of his, came in and made particular inquiry of his health. Adams answered, 'I inhabit a weak, frail, decayed tenement; battered by the winds and broken in upon by the storms, and, from all I can learn, the landlord does not intend to repair.'"

We miss out on a lot by not taking old people seriously. So nourish your soul. Don't merely go to visit someone who lives in a nursing home. Think about it. How would you feel in his or her situation? Would you enjoy sitting around a nursing home all day long, day after day, week after week, month after tedious month? Of course not.

First, connect with an older person who would enjoy a change of scenery now and then. It's the easiest thing in the world. All you need do is call a nearby nursing home and talk with someone on the staff. Just like that you will be introduced to an old person who would like to make a break for the outside world once a week or two or three times a month.

No need to make a big deal out of this. Maybe you have only an hour each time. Fine. Explain that you will be coming by at lunch time and you would like to take him or her to a fast food hamburger joint for a sandwich and a soft drink. Your new friend will look forward to that one-hour outing each week more than you can realize. When you get old yourself, you will understand. When you get old yourself.

Sometimes it seems as if we live in the era of whiners. Feeling sorry for oneself is fashionable and socially acceptable. In particular, blaming your parents for your own problems and unhappiness is totally *de rigueur.* If you are dissatisfied with your life it's your parents' fault. They didn't cultivate your self-esteem when you were a child. They botched your toilet training. They were authoritarian and they laid guilt trips on you. Your parents were mean to you, and your home life was terribly unhappy. Poor you.

Perhaps your father was a drunk who beat your mother, not to mention you and your brothers and sisters. Perhaps your mother was a hopeless alcoholic. Perhaps your parents divorced, depriving you of a healthy family life when you were a child. Maybe you didn't feel loved. Maybe nobody helped you with your homework and you had to do all the house work because your mother was too lazy.

The stories about unhappy growing up years are as countless as the grains of sand on the seashore. Get six people together and start them talking about their unhappy childhoods and before long the conversation takes on a "top this" spirit. You think you had an unhappy childhood? Listen to this.... The story will be a good one, no doubt, a real shocker, a regular orgy of self-pity.

Please stop. Nourish your soul. Stop blaming your parents for your apparent inability to hold a job. Stop blaming your parents for all your woes. Stop blaming your parents for everything that goes wrong with your life. Face it, they are/were only human. Like you. You seem to imply that they should have been perfect when you were a child. They are allowed no mistakes, no weaknesses, no sins.

Forgive your parents for what they did to you, whatever you know or think it was. Forgive your parents for getting divorced when you were a child. Forgive your mother for being a hopeless alcoholic. Forgive your father for never showing you how to work on a car or for never taking you fishing. Consider the experiences they had as children themselves.

Leonard Bernstein, the great American conductor, composer, and pianist, had a father like everyone else. Bernstein's father was criticized for not having given his talented son more encouragement when he was a child. He protested: "How was I to know he would grow up to be Leonard Bernstein?"

Parents have a difficult time thinking of their children as anything but children, and children are difficult sometimes. Your parents did the best they could. You were a child at the time. If you are a parent yourself, be honest. Are you a perfect parent?

75 ◆ *Confess Your Sins*

ONE OF THE ADVANTAGES of blaming your parents for your troubles (see #74) is that it lets you off the hook. If it's your parents' fault that you are unhappy, that means you need accept no responsibility. When you were lazy and got low grades or didn't finish school, it was your parents' fault. When you lost a job because you were regularly late for work, it was your parents' fault. And so on and so forth...

Think about your sins. You know what a sin is, right? A sin is any action that hurts you, your relationships with other people, or the earth. To do any of these things is to damage your relationship with your Creator, as well. If you make a choice that is harmful to you that's a sin. If you make a choice that hurts your relationship with your spouse, your children, or people you work with that's a sin. If you choose to do something that is harmful to the environment or the earth's ecological balance that's a sin, too. Pouring old oil from your car on the ground or into a storm drain qualifies.

You won't need to think about it for long before you come up with a tidy list of sins, choices that you are responsible for. Nobody else, just you. Now, nourish your soul by confessing your sins. Tell a person you trust what you did and say that you're sorry and will do your best not to do such things again. Listen to any advice the other person may wish to offer. Then go and tell the people you hurt that you're sorry, too.

If you happen to be a Roman Catholic or Eastern Orthodox Christian, you're in luck. Your religious tradition has a frequently used rite of confession and reconciliation you may take advantage of. Episcopalians and Lutherans also have such a ritual available, although they don't often use it. If you're a Lutheran or Episcopalian, go ahead and use it. You'll be glad you did.

If you belong to none of these traditions, you're on your own, but don't be discouraged. Sure, it makes good sense to simply confess your sins to God. But there is something powerful and tremendously healing about confessing your sins to another person. Get together with the person you wish to confess to. Plan a ritual. Maybe you would like to confess to each other.

You could begin with a scriptural or nonscriptural reading about forgiveness and mercy. Then recite your sins aloud. You could also write your sins on a piece of paper; then after reciting them put a match to the paper and burn it. Promise to "make amends" with anyone you may have hurt. Conclude with a prayer, formal or spontaneous.

Confessing your sins is a very grown-up thing to do.

76 ◆ *Take a Walk in a Summer Rain*

WE HAVE A THING about rain, many of us. Rain starts to fall and we run for shelter. We carry an umbrella and use it the minute the rain comes down. Sometimes all this avoidance makes sense — in cold times of the year, for example. Nobody needs pneumonia. But in the summer when rain falls on warm days, that's a different story altogether.

There is something pleasant about a summer rain. When you have the opportunity, go for walk in a warm summer rain. The minute the drops start coming down go outside with no umbrella and no hat or raincoat. Stand in the rain and let it fall into your face. Put your head back and look straight up at the rain falling down. Walk around and be a little bit childish. Step in some puddles and splash. Get soaking wet.

Rain is a blessing, not a misfortune. A warm summer rain is a sign of the benevolence of the universe and the Creator of the universe. It comes for free; you don't need to pay anyone for it. Rain brings life, enabling flowers and shrubs and trees to grow. Indeed, rain brings a new beauty to just about everything. Mark

Van Doren wrote a poem about it called "Rain Beautifies the City." Here it is:

> Rain beautifies the city;
> Makes mirrors of it, flattering
> Our minds, our eyes; even
> The Sparrows, resting, glance at themselves
> In windows and think they are cleaner
> For once; while cornices drip
> And gutters gurgle, and tires
> Hiss incessantly, saying
> Look, it is different now, listen
> And look, it is not the same
> City at all, it is old, old — an old
> Woman with bright eyes, remembering
> The youth of the world, the cool,
> The dancing feet, the flung capes, the morning
> Cries, the sun, the whistles, and the unkillable
> Hope, the unstoppable joy.

Walk in a warm summer rain, and allow yourself to receive its blessings. Don't curl into yourself, resisting. Instead, throw your arms wide, and your soul wide, and be completely open to the blessings of the summer rain. There is no other joy like this.

If possible, go for your walk in a summer rain with a child. Ideally, this child should be four or five years old. Watch the child and do as he or she does in the rain. Allow the rain to awaken joy in your soul. Allow the joy to be there. Laugh out loud, as the child does. Laugh out loud in the warm summer rain with your face turned up to receive the blessings of the rain.

Let the rain fall into your face and receive the baptism of joy. Let the rain fall into your face and receive the baptism of a completely new life.

77 ◆ Remember a Deceased Relative or Friend

YOU HAVE a relative or friend, someone you were close to, who is now deceased. Think about this person and about his or her life. If you have a photograph of this person, sit down and look at the photograph. Remember. What are your memories?

Death takes us all, but relationships...well, that's another matter. Something about relationships with those we love simply does not go away when death separates us. We still feel connected to deceased loved ones. In some way we can't quite put our finger on we still feel close. Is it not possible, then, that your deceased relative or friend still has some connection with you? Indeed, is it not possible that he or she is closer to you than you think?

Death is a mystery and a profound one. We know it happens but we don't know what happens. All we see is what ends. If something new begins it remains a hope, a theory, a hypothesis that can't be proven. And yet...and yet....What can we learn from our relationships, in particular our relationships with those who have died? If there is no afterlife, no better life after this life, why do we continue to feel close to deceased relatives and friends?

There is no proof that death is *not* the end. Neither is there any proof that death *is* the end. Only the heart can speak of such matters, so it's important that we listen to our heart and heed what it tells us. The heart has perceptions that the intellect knows nothing about, and we should trust those perceptions.

Look at the photograph of your deceased relative or friend. What might his or her life teach you about living your own life? So often we view life as a problem to be solved, a tough nut to crack. Rather, life is a mystery, a revelation, and a gift. Life is an opportunity. What did your deceased relative or friend do with that opportunity? What are you doing with it? Are there some changes you could and should make?

Now...talk to your deceased relative or friend. Use your ordinary speaking voice; don't just do it silently in your head. This is not a wacko idea, but you should probably do it in private when no one else can hear you lest there should be questions about your mental balance.

Talk to your deceased relative or friend. Tell this person how you see his or her life now that it is over. What meaning does it have for you now? Talk to him or her about your own life. Express your hopes and fears, but talk about what you're thankful for, as well. Tell your deceased relative or friend how things are going for you, for other loved ones still living, and in the world. Ask questions and leave them hanging in the air.

78 ◆ *Clarify Your Image of God*

WE ALL HAVE an image — or several images — of God. We carry these around in our mind and imagination. Even people who claim to be agnostics or atheists have images of the God whose existence they doubt or deny. They would have to say: here is the God I do not believe in or whose existence I doubt.

To begin with, we will assume that God is beyond the grasp of all human cognitive powers. Therefore, the first thing we must say about God is that we can say nothing. Fine. Given this first truth about God, we must also admit that we use the word "God" to refer to something or other. "God" is a word we use when we wish to talk about...what? The Supreme Being? The Creator? The Great Cosmic Wherewithal?

Let us call what we are talking about, for lack of a better term, "the Divine Mystery." This is as good as anything. Now, when you think of the Divine Mystery, or God, what is the main image you have in mind? Is God a Cosmic Policeman ready to pounce on you and punish you severely whenever you do something you should not? Or is God a kind of vacuous Cosmic Muffin that has no substantial place in your life at all?

Think back to your childhood. What are your earliest memories of God-talk? How did the adults in your life talk about God? What feelings about God did they pass on to you by the ways they talked and behaved when it came to things religious or philosophical? What are the connections between those early experiences and your current dominant image of God? How has your image of God changed over the years?

Here is the truth. If God is the absolutely incomprehensible Divine Mystery all we have are metaphors to understand this God. It's as simple and profound as that. So, which metaphors work best for you? "Father" is a metaphor. So is "Mother." "King," — as in "King of the Universe," is a metaphor, as are "Lord" and "Creator." Metaphors are all we have, and chances are that one metaphor will work best for you at some times while another metaphor will work better at other times.

Keep this uppermost in mind, however. Keep this uppermost in mind. No matter what metaphor you use for God,

God is always bigger than your metaphor. Don't take any of your metaphors for God too seriously. Sometimes people use metaphors for political reasons — insisting on feminine metaphors for God, for example, in order to promote a feminist political agenda among religious groups. Others insist on never using feminine metaphors for God, only masculine ones, in order to promote a contrary political agenda. Either approach could be called "metaphorolotry" — worship of a metaphor rather than God.

79 ◆ Like Yourself

SINCE THE 1960s there has been a huge amount of hype about the importance of healthy self-esteem. It could be that this bred an inordinate enthusiasm for the so-called Human Potential Movement and the jargon of pop psychology. It could very well be.

That said, the basic insight remains true. If you don't like yourself how do you expect anyone else to like you? A young woman participated in a weekend retreat, and everyone could see that on one of her legs she wore a prosthesis from the knee down. Also, the fingers on one of her hands were not fully developed. Her body never fully developed before she was born.

This young woman had reasons to not like herself. Imagine the rejection and cruelty she must have suffered from other children when she was growing up. Yet for whatever reason she was quite comfortable with herself and with being around a rather large group of other people she had never met before. The weather was sunny and warm. She was wearing shorts and sandals so her prosthesis was evident to everyone, and it took only a moment for others to notice her hands. Yet this young woman smiled, laughed easily, and interacted with the other people on the retreat with no inhibitions at all. Clearly, she liked herself, and before long so did everyone else.

Nourish your soul by liking yourself. Everyone has flaws, imperfections, weaknesses, foibles, idiosyncrasies. Everyone makes mistakes; everyone does something stupid now and then. No big deal. You are above average, you have good ideas, and you are creative.

Talk like this may not seem helpful. You can give yourself positive messages until you choke on them, and it may not help you feel any better about yourself. What can you do then?

It is the rare person who arrives at adulthood without some wounds to his or her self-esteem. We all need some healing. Books and counselors can offer practical help. But one of the best ways to like yourself more is to expose yourself to God's unconditional love for you. This is something you have complete control over, and here is how it works.

Spend ten minutes a day in whatever form of silent meditation works best for you. An excellent approach is to close your eyes, sit still, be quiet, and repeat over and over in your mind a one-line prayer or devotional truth. "God, come into my heart and fill me with your love." Any short prayer will do, and if you do this every day it will have a healing effect on your feelings about yourself. The more you become aware of God's love for you the more you will have a healthy love for yourself.

80 ◆ *Choose Your Own Destiny*

MANY PEOPLE feel that they have little control over their lives. In reality, no one has more control than you do. You are in charge of your own destiny in this world, regardless of the conditions you face. You can't always choose what happens to you, but you can choose what to do about what happens to you. That is a freedom and a power no one can take away from you. Nourish your soul by choosing your own destiny.

If you are young, "footloose and fancy free," you may wonder about what to do with your life. Perhaps you would like to get married, but there are no prospects on the horizon. Realize this, that healthy, lasting marriages happen when you are living your life as you should. If you are doing what you should be doing, you will meet someone who will make a good spouse.

Sometimes young people make marriage their main goal. They think that if they get married this will resolve their identity problem. In fact, it works the other way around. If you figure out who you are, what you believe in, and the work or career you want, marriage will take care of itself. People who already know who they are marry successfully. People who are still trying to figure out the meaning of life often do not marry successfully. It's that simple.

If you are somewhere in midlife, chances are you have mixed feelings about your life. Ambiguity City, and that's normal. You have already made the big decisions about whether to marry and who to marry, you already have or do not have children, and the future seems rather predictable. It's true that you have already mapped out your future in some major ways. All the same, you still have considerable control over what the future will bring.

What are your main concerns? More years working after the kids are grown and gone, then a comfortable retirement with financial security, then eventually you croak? Is that your plan? Is this a destiny you are excited about, that you look forward to with enthusiasm? If so, fine. But what if, through no fault of your own, you do not have the economic freedom you planned on? Then what? What are your alternate choices?

Is the most important thing in life economic security? Will that really make you happy? Are there other things in life you can plan to do that will enable you to get along financially but will fill your life with more of an adventure than you used to think retirement would bring? Are you up for an adventure in your life after the kids are gone?

What kind of destiny do you want? A dull one or an exciting one? What do you want to have in life? An adventure or a nap?

81 ◆ *Be Optimistic*

I N *Bleak House*, by Charles Dickens, there is a character named Mr. Smallweed whose family prides itself on being grim. Dickens describes the Smallweed family thus:

The house of Smallweed, always early to go out and late to marry, has strengthened itself in its practical character, has discarded all amusements, discountenanced all story-books, fairy-tales, fictions, and fables, and banished all levities whatsoever. Hence the gratifying fact that it has had no child born to it and that the complete little men and women whom it has produced have been observed to bear a likeness to old monkeys with something depressing on their minds.

Dickens offers here a fine portrayal of a pessimistic outlook, and if a pessimistic outlook guarantees anything it guarantees a depressing life. You can count on it.

Nourish your soul. Be optimistic. Optimism is a virtue, that is, a source of strength and vitality. At the same time, optimism is not always easy. Sometimes it can be difficult. Indeed, being optimistic is difficult while being pessimistic is easy, just as faith is difficult while skepticism and unbelief are the easiest things in the world.

Sometimes you need to work at being optimistic. Strange as it may sound, sometimes hope takes work. You may need to resist the inclination toward pessimism. Many studies show that optimists are healthier and live longer. Instead of viewing setbacks as signs of failure see them as accidental flukes or as opportunities to try something different. If you think positively you will have positive outcomes. If you think negatively you will have negative outcomes.

Cultivate optimism by reading stories about people you admire who overcame great odds to go on and attain their goals. Actor Jim Carrey tells of spending time thinking of himself as a huge success. Years before he made his first movie he wrote himself a huge check for making a movie that had not been made yet. A few years later he received twice as much for making a real movie.

What do you want to have happen in your life? Visualize that event as actually happening. Think of yourself as that kind of person. The world simply hasn't caught up with you yet. Then go on striving toward your goal, whatever it may be. Cultivate optimism, but do it in an unselfish manner. Be optimistic but not in a self-centered fashion. Think, rather, about those you want to be successful for — your family or other people you want to help by your success.

Expect good things to happen, not bad things. Do not look like an old monkey with something depressing on your mind.

PHYSICAL FITNESS can be a fad or it can be a way of life. In order to nourish your soul it needs to be a way of life. This does not mean you must become an Olympic-class athlete. It does not mean you must eat only the kinds of foods to be found in health food stores. It does not mean you must never eat meat, confining yourself to nuts and berries. It does mean taking seriously your need for balanced nutrition and regular exercise. For what you do to your body you do to your soul.

Nourish your soul with a healthy diet. A vegetarian diet is good, but you can eat meat and fowl and fish and still be healthy. Eat plenty of vegetables, fruits, and grains. Eat whole grain breads. Most of the time stay away from a deep fried fast-food diet high in saturated fat. Keep your consumption of refined sugar low.

Eat salads. Chicken is okay as long as it's not fried. Avoid the skin of the chicken. Fish is good as long as it's not deep fried. If you are over the age of ten, forget about drinking cow's milk. Well, a bit on cereal in the morning is acceptable since many people find it difficult to take their oatmeal without milk. Break-fast cereals you must cook are always better, and less expensive, than ready-to-eat cold cereals, most of which contain enough sugar to strangle the Sugar Plum Fairy. If you enjoy red meat, include it rarely and then make it low in fat. Buy ground beef with the lowest fat content available.

Drink bottled waters rather than sugar-saturated soft drinks. Keep your caffeine consumption low, which means not only coffee but regular tea and many soft drinks. Herbal teas are good.

Smoking sucks, and chewing tobacco is disgusting. Does anyone not know that chewing tobacco causes mouth cancer and smoking will kill you faster than any other nasty addiction you can think of? The cigarette industry ought to be marched into the courtyard and shot at sunrise for what it continues to foist on teenagers through its insidious advertising campaigns and cultivation of peer pressure to smoke.

Drug abuse is obviously counterproductive. Alcohol is bad news, although the occasional glass of wine with dinner, or the occasional beer for the simple pleasure of it will do you no damage. Hard liquor seems unnecessary, but go ahead once in a great while if you must. Just watch it around the kids, okay?

Exercise regularly in whatever way you enjoy. Bicycle riding is fun. Many people enjoy jogging or walking. Join a fitness club if that works for you and gets you to work up a sweat three times a week. Take up a martial art. Get an exercise bike or treadmill. Then actually use it.

83 ◆ *Be Outgoing*

SOCIABLE, OUTGOING PEOPLE get more out of life. They have more friends, and they live longer. Other people enjoy being around someone who is cheerful and high-spirited. If you work at being extroverted you will find your days more pleasant and joy-filled.

It's true that you have a genetically established basic disposition. It's also true that social forces in our lives shape our personality as we grow up. *But it is also true that we have the power to shape our own destinies.* For we are not only the creatures of our social and spiritual world but the creators of it. We are not only the product of our past but the builders of our future. We are not rigidly determined as absolute behaviorists would have us believe. The predispositions we bring into the world leave room to be influenced by our family background and childhood social experiences. They also leave room for our own efforts. You have the power to take action today in order to shape your life tomorrow.

So work at being more outgoing, because to a great extent your feelings and attitudes will follow your behavior. Just because you don't feel outgoing does not mean that you cannot act in an outgoing fashion. Nourish your soul by changing your behavior and you will be surprised at how your feelings and attitudes will change, too. This may feel phony at first, but your feelings will gradually change as your outgoingness becomes genuine. Going through the motions will spark positive, hopeful, outgoing emotions.

The great comedian Jimmy Durante (1893–1980) began his

career with another great, the singer Eddie Cantor. When the two were singing and playing together in cafés, Cantor would encourage Durante to quit playing the piano and try something more ambitious on the vaudeville stage.

"I know you want to be a piano player," Cantor said, "but piano playing is going to get you nothing. You'll be a piano player till you're a hundred years old. You gotta look further than that. People like you a whole lot. So why don't you get up on the floor and say something to the people? Make remarks while you're playing the piano?"

To this Jimmy answered, "Gee, Eddie, I couldn't do that. I'd be afraid people would laugh at me."

All the same, Jimmie Durante took Eddie Cantor's advice, and his large nose earned him the title "the Great Schnozzola." He became one of the great entertainers of the twentieth century because he decided to act more outgoing even though he didn't feel that way. Jimmy Durante became his true self by acting in a way he was not comfortable with at first.

84 ◆ *Cultivate Friendships*

WE ARE MADE for friendship, and nothing nourishes the soul like having friends. So cultivate friendships. How do you make friends? You do this by being a friend. A friend is someone who appreciates you for who you are, not for what you do. Start small; find someone who needs a friend and become that person's friend.

The Bible says: "Faithful friends are a sturdy shelter: whoever finds one has found a treasure. Faithful friends are beyond price; no amount can balance their worth. Faithful friends are life-saving medicine; and those who fear the Lord will find them" (Sirach 6:14–16).

Of course, if you find someone who needs a friend it's possible that person will be someone who has difficulty attracting friends. But once you become a person's friend that person becomes more attractive as a potential friend for others, as well.

Lord George Gordon Byron, the early nineteenth-century

English poet, was born with a "clubfoot," which medical science could do nothing about in those days. While Byron and his friend Robert Peel were schoolmates, one day Byron saw Peel being beaten unmercifully by a senior boy. It was hopeless for Byron to think of fighting because of his crippled foot. All the same, he approached the bully and bravely inquired how many times he was planning on striking his friend. "What's that to you?" the bully roared. "Because, if you please," Byron replied, trembling with rage and fear, "I would take half."

A friend is one who would do something like this. A friend is not just someone to pal around with. True friendship means knowing as you are known. Friends know they can be their true selves with one another; no need to "put on an act."

Friendship is even more than this, however. The ideal is to have friends and no enemies. During the Civil War Abraham Lincoln, at an official function, referred to the Southerners not as foes to be exterminated but as erring human beings. An elderly lady, intensely patriotic, rebuked Lincoln for speaking kindly of his enemies when he ought to be thinking of destroying them. "Why, madam," Lincoln said, "do I not destroy my enemies when I make them my friends?"

Sometimes old friends are the best friends. But sometimes old friends are also distant friends, and we don't stay in touch as often as we might. So nourish your soul by getting in touch more often with old friends. The relatively recent phenomenon of e-mail may revive the dying art of letter writing. Write to some old friends, letting them know how important they are to you.

85 ◆ Be Chaste

OUR ERA frequently snickers at the ideal of chastity. The very idea that one should reserve sexual activity for marriage may seem quaint, at best. "Living together" before — or instead of — marriage is more and more common. Sexual activity among teenagers is not unusual, although surveys indicate that more than 60 percent of teenagers are *not* sexually active.

Chastity as an ideal borders on the hilarious in the popular culture, so the idea that you can nourish your soul by being chaste may strike you as odd or downright bizarre. Such a reaction may stem from misunderstanding. According to a dictionary of spirituality, "Chastity is the moral virtue referring to the adoption of ethical and moral norms that moderate and regulate the sexual appetite.... Although sexual self-moderation is an absolute value, historical and cultural studies indicate that the practice of chastity has varied in various times and places and that it is subject to differing sociological conditions."

What does it mean here and now to be chaste? We're not talking about rigid Victorian attitudes toward sex. We don't live in the nineteenth century. We are talking about sexual behavior that shows respect for oneself and others. We are also talking about sexual behavior that is appropriate to "the big picture," if you will, sexual behavior that fits the situation.

There is a difference between a couple of teenagers groping in the back of a car and a young couple who will be married next week. All the same, there is much to be said in favor of the traditional prohibition against sexual intercourse outside of marriage. Being chaste means reserving the total physical gift of oneself to another until the relationship as a whole embodies a total, unconditional commitment.

The commitment of a man and woman to each other is not complete until it is made public in a wedding ceremony. Therefore, it is inappropriate for the couple to share themselves completely with each other until that public commitment is made. Chastity precludes sexual intercourse before marriage because sexual intercourse is inappropriate until after the wedding. It may also be harmful to the relationship.

Several sociological studies during the 1980s and 1990s indicate that the divorce rate among couples who "lived together" prior to marriage is about 50 percent higher than among couples who chose a traditional dating relationship until they were married. Chastity is not a hang-up. It is an expression of common sense, respect, and good will.

After marriage, chastity means sharing sexual pleasure often but only with your spouse. So nourish your soul by being chaste in the way that suits your situation.

86 ◆ *Be Angry in Appropriate Ways*

IN A CONTEMPORARY CLASSIC, *Wishful Thinking*, Frederick Buechner wrote with captivating insight about the negative side of anger:

> Of the Seven Deadly Sins, anger is possibly the most fun. To lick your wounds, to smack your lips over grievances long past, to roll over your tongue the prospect of bitter confrontations still to come, to savor to the last toothsome morsel both the pain you are given and the pain you are giving back — in many ways it is a feast fit for a king. The chief drawback is that what you are wolfing down is yourself. The skeleton at the feast is you.

But anger is sometimes not a self-destructive emotion. Sometimes it can spark actions on behalf of truth and justice. One of the best-known examples of what we might call "righteous anger" occurs in a story in the Christian Scriptures about the anger of Jesus of Nazareth.

> Again he entered the synagogue, and a man was there who had a withered hand. They [i.e. the Pharisees] watched him to see whether he would cure him on the sabbath, so that they might accuse him. And he said to the man who had the withered hand, "Come forward." Then he said to them, "Is it lawful to do good or to do harm on the sabbath, to save life or to kill?" But they were silent. *He looked around at them with anger;* he was grieved at their hardness of heart and said to the man, "Stretch out your hand." He stretched it out, and his hand was restored. (Mark 3:1–5; emphasis added)

The Pharisees are more concerned about observance of religious legalisms than they are about human needs. They are ready to pounce on Jesus if he violates a religious law in order to carry out an act of mercy. Jesus is angry with the Pharisees for their hardness of heart. Notice, Jesus is angry, but he does not allow his anger to push him into violence. Rather, his anger prompts him to do what is right with no regard for what the Pharisees may think or do, no thought of possible negative consequences for himself.

Anger is hot. Anger burns like a fire, and like a fire it can be either a friend or an enemy. Either way, anger is dangerous and is best handled carefully. "Anger is never without a reason," said Benjamin Franklin, "but seldom with a good one." "People who fly into a rage always make a bad landing," said Will Rogers.

It is so easy to justify anger, especially if it results from a perceived offense to yourself. But, says an old proverb, "Anger is
often more hurtful than the injury that caused it." In truth, there
is only one justification for anger, and that is evil or sin. If you
would be angry and not sin, follow the example of Jesus and
never be angry with anything except sin.

Yes, we all feel angry at times. The best action to take when
you feel anger because of some perceived offense to yourself is
to beat the stuffing out of a pillow. Get it out without hurting
yourself or anyone else.

87 ◆ *Get a Massage*

W E LIVE in stressful times, we beneficiaries of the great
technological advances of the modern age. Our lives are
filled with time-saving gadgets, but we don't seem to have
enough time. Our lives are filled with hurry and pressure. At
the end of the day the muscles in our neck and back are tense
and tight. We need someone to give us a good massage. Human
touch from a qualified massage therapist can nourish the soul
like nothing else in this world.

We touch children when they are hurt, we give them hugs
and kiss them when they cry, but we don't do this for adults.
Adults come home from work and use alcohol to relax when
what they need is someone to sooth and touch them, to melt
away the stress.

Chances are you live in your head all day and become discon-
nected from your body. Massage is about the body and regaining
awareness of the physical self. A good massage brings awareness
back to your whole self. During a massage you may remember
things you had forgotten, or emotions may surface you don't
expect. Often, people have been hurt through touch, possibly
physical or sexual abuse as a child or as an adult. Massage is a
healing form of touch. It says that your body is good and worthy
of respect.

Often people avoid massage because they have hatred for their
own body. They don't want to expose themselves to another

human being. But during a massage hatred for the body dissolves. The massage therapist's hands remind you that you are good and beautiful.

Sometimes people hardly ever get touched at all. This can be true for older people, especially widowed people. They experience physical — and so spiritual — impoverishment from lack of human touch. Older people also often have numerous aches and pains, and massage can be a relief.

Massage connects you with your whole self, body and soul. One form of massage, called Reflexology, sees connections between various parts of your feet and the other parts of your body. The small area between and just below the second and third toes connects to the eye, for example, while the middle of the heel relates to the knee and hip areas. Massage of the foot can benefit the entire body.

Massage connects you with your deeper self. On the massage table you may go into a quiet space you rarely experience otherwise. Massage opens a door that may remain closed at all other times. You enter a soft, open space in yourself. So nourish your soul by getting a massage.

88 ◆ Allow Yourself to Be Awestruck

WE ARE SO JADED. Been there, done that, seen that. No more surprises, no more wonders. When Charles Lindbergh crossed the Atlantic Ocean alone in his little airplane, *The Spirit of St. Louis,* no one had ever done that before. People were awestruck, and Lindbergh became a hero. When the first human beings traveled tentatively into space, people were impressed, and when the first human walked on the moon they were amazed. But something has happened. Nothing knocks our socks off anymore.

Nourish your soul by allowing yourself to be awestruck. Don't worry that others may think you naive. Look into the face of a newborn infant and be awestruck. Go backpacking and climb to the top of a forested mountain. Stand on top of that mountain and be awestruck at the splendor of the scene spread out before you on all sides.

Get away from the artificial lights that beat back the nighttime darkness in cities. Go out into the countryside on a cloudless night, someplace where there are no artificial lights. Spread out a blanket on the ground, lie down on the blanket, and look up at the stars. Give yourself permission to be awestruck. It's okay.

Ask yourself about the orderliness of it all, the constellations spinning through space, our own planet but a speck in the vast and starry Milky Way. Allow yourself to feel some awe in the face of it all. Say things a child might say: "Wow!" "Awesome!" Allow yourself to feel overwhelmed by it all.

If you are in an airplane flying into a big city, look out the window at the skyscrapers below and feel some awe at what the human mind and human hands have accomplished. Think what it took to build such a city. Recall that 150 years ago — a mere blip in history — this same city was downright pastoral by comparison. "Wow!"

Stand before a mirror. Don't be shy. Look at your own face, into your own eyes. Say, "Who am I? What am I? Where did I come from? Why do I look different now than I did ten years ago? What's happening?" Things like that. Feel some awe about the mystery of it all. Allow yourself to be ever so slightly awestruck.

89 ◆ *Join an Institutional Religion*

As far as the dominant popular culture is concerned, "institutional religion" is in bad taste. Only those unable to cope with reality take refuge in "institutional religion," people who need a spiritual crutch. "Spirituality" may be popular, but who would want to have anything to do with "institutional religion." We would rather put together our own spiritual outlook on life and the world, something unique to fit our unique self.

There is something charmingly naive about this popular perspective. It's also charmingly American, an echo of that good old

American individualism we all know so well. We will do it on our own, by damn, and everybody else better leave us alone.

In a book called *Through a Glass Darkly: A Spiritual Psychology of Faith*, author Mary Jo Meadow writes: "Religious institutions seem to be a 'necessary evil' when it comes to faith. They help transmit spiritual truths, but often limit seekers' perspectives in ways that block spiritual growth and obscure spiritual truths....

"Let the question become: of all the worthy paths that have brought people to God, which is or are the best for me at this time?"

How utterly broad-minded, wouldn't you say? For this perspective the subjective individual is an absolute. You should measure all of life and all the universe according to your own personal, subjective, private measure at this moment in time. Indeed, you are the measure of all truth, beauty, and goodness. There are no objective truths, only what's meaningful for you.

This is a summary of the most popular perspective on spirituality and religions today. But it overlooks something. Granted that religious institutions have their faults and weaknesses, and sometimes religious leaders are arrogant and self-serving, does this mean that I — me, myself, and I — constitute an infallible authority? Is it not remotely possible that "institutional religions" exist because historically people found them necessary and, in the long run, more worthwhile than not, more expanding than limiting? Is it not possible that an institutional religion can help me to nourish my spirituality in ways I might never discover on my own, thrashing about to put together my own little eclectic spiritual mix?

To refuse allegiance to any single institutional religion is to hold oneself aloof from full membership in and commitment to any human religious community at all. It is to make a career of standing on the sidelines.

Nourish your soul. Join an institutional religion. There you will find fulfillment, meaning, and spiritual truth. You will also find frustration, narrow-mindedness, and conflict. Welcome to the human race.

90 ◆ *Turn Off (or Throw Out) Your Television Set*

J UST TRY to put together a cogent defense of television. Reasons to not watch television are legion. Reasons to watch it are few. One of the Almighty Tube's most articulate critics is Neil Postman, author of *The Disappearance of Childhood* and *Amusing Ourselves to Death*. Another is Jerry Mander, who wrote *Four Arguments for the Elimination of Television*. A third is Marie Winn, author of *The Plug-In Drug: Children, Television, and the Family*. Finally, there is Jim Trelease, who wrote a terrific chapter on television in *The Read-Aloud Handbook*.

Neil Postman, professor of media ecology at New York University, argues that television is responsible for exposing children to the same information as adults, to the point that the boundaries between childhood and adulthood hardly exist anymore. He suggests that nothing makes it onto television unless it is entertaining, and that includes the most highly respected news programs. The most newsworthy events often don't make it to the evening news because they have no "entertainment value."

Jerry Mander, formerly president of a major San Francisco advertising firm, insists that television's problems belong to the nature of the technology itself and are so dangerous, to personal health and sanity, to the environment, and to democratic processes, that television should be eliminated. Period. Forever.

Marie Winn, a family issues author, declares that the passive act of watching television has a negative effect on the developing child's relationship to the real world. It also has a destructive effect on family relationships and educational processes.

Jim Trelease, a former journalist and authority on the benefits of reading aloud to children, does not support throwing out your television set. But what he says about television may inspire you to do so all the same. He discusses at length how to cope with the negative powers of television in the home. Among Trelease's criticisms of television are these: Television deprives the child of his or her most important learning tool, which is questions. Television is unable to portray the most intelligent human act, which is thinking. Television encourages deceptive thinking. Television stifles the imagination.

Nourish your soul by not watching television or by watching it only on rare occasions. Choose instead some of the other activities suggested in this book. There is rarely anything on television you can't get in a superior form through the print media or live performances.

Thomas Merton once said that watching TV could easily become a dangerous form of pseudocontemplative prayer. Don't let it happen.

91 ◆ *Make Your Own Ice Cream*

THERE IS SOMETHING about ice cream that evokes the spirit not just of childhood but of a carefree spirit at any age. If you make the ice cream yourself it tastes even better because you work rather strenuously first. The ice cream is the reward for your labors.

On a hot summer day, get yourself an ice cream maker — not an electrified one, that's cheating. Get one you must hand crank. Mix the ingredients, the cream, the sugar, the fruit or chocolate syrup if you wish, all those ingredients that are on the danger list when it comes to fat and cholesterol. Just looking at them is liable to turn your aorta into a hockey puck. Mix them all up, pour them into the ice cream maker, and pour the ice chunks between the inner cylinder containing the ingredients and the outside wall of the ice cream maker. Sprinkle rock salt on the ice. Now start cranking. Invite friends and be sure everyone takes a turn cranking, turning the crank, turning and turning, until finally...you have thick, rich, highly fattening ice cream. Serve it up in cones or bowls. Savor the flavor, a flavor and a pleasure to die for.

The ice-cream-making project nourishes the soul even before you get to eat the ice cream. It nourishes the soul because from beginning to end it's a group process, putting together the ingredients, mixing them up, getting them into the ice cream maker, turning the crank, it's all for one and one for all. The eating is a pleasure that celebrates the group effort, and both the making and the eating nourish the soul. Such deep, rich pleasure on the tongue inspires sheer, mindless gratitude at the simple fact of being alive and being with friends.

92 ◆ *Memorize a Prayer*

TIME WAS, children had to memorize prayers, Bible verses, the answers to catechism questions. It was part of their religious formation. If you memorized something religious it stuck with you, and when you needed it there it would be, lodged in your mind and heart. That was the theory. Maybe it wasn't the best theory in the world, but it wasn't the worst, either. There is something to be said for memorizing a few prayers.

Sometimes you need to pray, but you can't think of what to say on the spur of the moment. You find yourself grateful for a formal memorized prayer to use when your heart is so overwhelmed — with joy, or pain, or boredom — that spontaneous just doesn't work. So nourish your soul by memorizing a prayer.

Time was, it was no big deal to memorize the entire Book of Psalms, all one hundred fifty, and some of them, Psalm 119 for example, are very, very long. Okay, maybe you don't want to tackle the entire Book of Psalms. You could do it if you wanted to, no question about that. But start slow and easy. Perhaps you already have a favorite psalm. For many people that would be the famous Psalm 23, "The LORD is my shepherd...." Maybe that's a good reason to choose a different one, something you're not so familiar with that may awaken newness in your heart when you pray it. Consider Psalm 9: "I will give thanks to the LORD with my whole heart; I will tell of all your wonderful deeds...."

Memorize it, line by line. First you memorize the first line, then you memorize the second line. That's two lines you have memorized. Now the third line, adding lines one by one until you have the whole prayer down pat. Say it at least once each day for a week or two, and it will be yours for life.

Traditional prayers seem to lend themselves best to memorization, and often it's the "all-purpose prayer" that seems most memorizable. Roman Catholics find the "Hail Mary" appropriate in many situations. Eastern Orthodox Christians may rely often on the silent "Jesus Prayer," a short but mystical prayer in its origins: "Lord Jesus Christ, Son of God, have mercy on me, a sinner."

Jewish tradition offers a plethora of prayers and blessings for all kinds of occasions, and Islam, with its tradition of prayer several times a day, requires the pious one to have memorized prayers to draw upon.

Sometimes, however, it can be both refreshing and delightful to memorize a contemporary, unpredictable prayer. Take one from one of Australian Michael Leunig's little collections of original prayers, for example. Here is one from *The Prayer Tree:*

> Dear God,
> we rejoice and give thanks
> for earthworms, bees, ladybirds and broody hens;
> for humans tending their gardens,
> talking to animals,
> cleaning their homes
> and singing to themselves;
> for the rising sap,
> the fragrance of growth,
> the invention of the wheelbarrow
> and the existence of the teapot,
> we give thanks.
> We celebrate and give thanks.
> Amen.

93 ◆ *Ponder the Eternal Verities*

WE GET CAUGHT UP in the thousand and one details and pressures of everyday life. We do. Hither and thither. Places to go, people to meet, things to do. That's life. Now and then, therefore, it nourishes the soul if we pause in the course of our day's occupations to ponder the eternal verities. Ponder those ultimate questions. Such as: Where did I come from? Why am I here? Where am I going? Little questions like that....

These three short questions require answers of an ultimate nature. The answers we give summarize our convictions about the meaning of life. Do you believe you brought yourself into being?

This means you have an ego the size of the World Trade Center in New York City.

Do you believe your parents, unassisted, abandoning themselves to biological urges and subject to subsequent purely biological processes, brought you into being? This means you will have a very tough time with the second and third questions.

Or do you believe you were brought into being by a benevolent Creator? In this case, you will be better prepared to figure out why you are here and the nature of your ultimate destiny.

We do not consider such matters as often as we should. We act as if life is all about getting and spending, eating and sleeping, entertaining ourselves and planning for retirement, raising the kids and surviving their adolescence. The last item is closer to the mark, but it still is no bull's eye. Honest, now. Where do you believe you came from? Write your answer here:

_____

Why do you believe you are here? Write your answer here:

_____

What do you think will happen to you after you die? Write your answer here:

_____

To get the most out of this little exercise, discuss your responses with another person. If that other person is your spouse, the discussion will not only nourish your soul, it will nourish your marriage, as well.

Once you ponder your answers to these basic questions about the meaning of life, ask yourself to what extent the way you actually live is consistent with the answers you gave.

94 ◆ *Soak in a Hot Tub*

FILL THE TUB with water just as hot as you like it. Maybe pour in some aromatic bath oil. Now get into the tub. Take your clothes off first. As the legendary disk jockey Wolfman Jack used to say: "Get nekkid!" Now get into the tub. Slide down into the comfort of the hot water, right up to your neck. Close your eyes. Take a deep breath and sigh audibly. What a relief....

There is something primordial about this experience. You feel lighter in the water. You bob a bit. Let the tension drain away. Remain as motionless as possible. There is something luxurious about soaking in the tub, and you don't need to be fabulously wealthy to enjoy this luxury.

Ernst Theodor Wilhelm Hoffmann, an early nineteenth-century novelist, composer, and theatrical manager, was once the guest of a newly rich acquaintance who liked to show off his recently gained wealth. After dinner the *nouveau riche* showed Hoffmann around his lavishly decorated house. Speaking of his servants, the millionaire remarked casually that he required three for his personal attendants. Hoffmann, a master of one-up-manship, replied that he had four just to take care of his daily bath: one to lay out the towels, one to test the temperature of the water, and a third to make sure the faucets were in good order.

"And the fourth?"

"Oh," said Hoffmann, "he's the most important of all. He takes my bath for me."

Har-dee-har-har. But Hoffmann missed out on the best part. Soaking in a hot bath, your eyes closed, is the sheerest heaven. It is a great way to free yourself from the day you just had, or a great way to prepare yourself for the day you're about to have. Either way, you're stronger and more resilient for the experience.

A bath — a shower, too, for that matter — can be an experience of near rebirth. We come out smelling like a rose, as fresh as a new-born babe. The person who gets out of the bath is not the person who got into the bath. Let the newness of your body after a bath or shower reflect the newness of your soul.

95 ◆ *Travel Off the Beaten Path*

HENRY DAVID THOREAU is best known, of course, as the early nineteenth-century author of the great American classic *Walden,* a book written after the author lived for some time in a

tiny cabin near Walden Pond, in Massachusetts. One day someone asked Thoreau whether he had traveled much, and Thoreau
replied, "Yes — around Concord."

Indeed, Henry David Thoreau traveled far more than most
people do without ever being far from his home town. There is
traveling widely, and there is traveling in depth, and the latter
has advantages over the former.

There are other differences in travel, as well. Many people
travel by joining a tour, a group of people guided every step of
the way by someone from a travel agency. Hotel reservations are
made in advance, plans are made, everything is arranged for. All
you need do is keep up and do as you're told. No surprises. You
see "all the right places." The idea is to broaden your perspective,
get a more cosmopolitan view of the world. Which is fine.

Other travelers decide to do it all on their own. They buy an
airplane ticket and go, ready to cope with the details as the need
arises. They make sleeping arrangements as they go, follow the
drift, perhaps end up staying in the homes of people they meet
along the way. This has advantages, too. You see other countries
and cultures in a haphazard way, willy-nilly as you may.

There is yet a third way. The idea is to see not just the tourist
spots or the people you encounter along the way. The idea is to
see the places tourists wouldn't want to see and countries, or parts
of countries, that will broaden your vision, you bet, but maybe
not as you expected. Travel on this plan is travel to see, literally,
how the other half — three-quarters is more like it — lives.

You go to countries in the Caribbean such as Jamaica, but
you avoid the plush hotels and fancy resorts. Instead, you drive
around to the other side of the island and see the poverty, people
who live on a vast garbage dump. You go to Central America
and see how people live in Guatemala or El Salvador. You travel
to Eastern Europe and see how you like the lifestyle there in the
wake of the fall of Communism. Or try mainland China, still in
the midst of its own helter-skelter Communist experiment.

Travel according to this third approach is to educate yourself
about how wealthy you are without realizing it. It will nourish
your soul. But be careful. It could change your life as well. You
may find yourself wanting to live in different ways than you lived
before.

96 ◆ *Cultivate a Garden*

MAYBE YOU HAVE a green thumb, maybe you don't. Either way, it can nourish your soul to plant and care for a garden of your own. It can be a very small garden or a very big one. It can be a garden in your back yard or an apartment-dweller's garden in a wooden tub. Your garden could be some distance from your home in a city-sponsored public garden area.

Regardless, the point is to nourish your soul by cultivating tomatoes, lettuce, and corn, or flowers of as many kinds as you like. You prepare the ground, digging it up, loosening the soil, getting it ready. You plant the seeds or set out the already started plants, as with tomatoes. You fertilize, you water, and you weed. You get down on your knees and work the earth, and one day the veggies and flowers you planted begin to poke up into the world above ground. Tomatoes like lots of sun.

You are a part of the earth. To cultivate the earth and make things grow is a primordial human activity. To cultivate the earth gets you into contact with basic forces, basic energies, clean, fresh, beautiful things.

It does something good for the soul to look a newly dug potato in the eye. It does something good for the soul to bake a rhubarb pie using rhubarb you grew yourself. It does something good for the soul to fill a basket with six or seven large zucchini, take them to a friend's house, leave them by the front door, ring the doorbell, and run back to your car and drive away ... (heh, heh, heh).

97 ◆ *Spend More Time Loafing*

YOU COULD START OUT by meditating upon more wisdom from Henry David Thoreau: "Simplify, simplify, let your concerns be as two or three...." That wouldn't be a bad idea. But maybe the following advice from James Thurber would be better: "It is better to have loafed and lost than never to have loafed at all."

Nourish your soul by simplifying your life, and the first step in simplifying your life is to loaf more than you ever loafed before.

This is not as easy as it may sound. Not by a far cry. If you are going to loaf more you will need to work less, and if you work less you will need to cut back on expenses because you probably won't have as much money. See, even simplifying your life can be complicated.

Do you like the work you do to pay the bills? If so, you're lucky. But if you are going to simplify your life you will need to spend less time doing it, whatever it is. Make up your mind to that right away or you won't get to first base, simpler-life-wise. What is the limit on the number of hours you are willing to work each day? Eight? Six? Whatever it is, decide on that and resolve to work no more than this, not even if your employer offers you three times your usual wage to do so. In your ear, three times the usual wage. That's the spirit. Because you are going to simplify your life, you can live on what you earn working eight hours a day.

Do you not like the work you do? Bummer. Until you find work you like, however, this has one advantage. You will feel less inclined to work overtime, even if your employer, the cad, offers you time-and-a-half. Put in your eight hours per, get the heck out of there, and get back to the loafing that is so basic to a simpler lifestyle. Loaf with your spouse if you're married, loaf with your kids if you have kids. Spend as much time as possible loafing. Make trips to the grocery store or hardware store only when absolutely unavoidable.

Note, however, that you should be sure to read suggestion #90 above, about strictly limiting your television watching. Authentic loafing is highly incompatible with television watching. Television short-circuits the loafing spirit and turns it into mere mind- and soul-numbing inertia. Bad news.

The usual translation of the Christian Scriptures tells us that "God is love." Recently, however, certain Pooh-esque scholars questioned the standard translation of the original Greek text. They suggest that this is the result of a textual corruption. Properly researched, they say, the text should read, "God is loaf[ing]." This puts the whole Christian religion in an entirely new light, of course. If God is loaf[ing], this means that it becomes highly virtuous to loaf. To loaf is God-like, even. The central Christian teaching would become: You shall loaf [like]

God with your whole self and loaf [with] your neighbor as [with] yourself.

Either way, however, to err is human, to loaf divine. So nourish your soul by loafing more.

98 ◆ *Clean House*

SOMETIMES the most mundane activities can have the most profound impact on the soul. Take eating a pizza, for example. You wouldn't believe what this can do for your soul. Or a thick, rich chocolate milkshake. Or cleaning house. Yes, cleaning house. This does not sound like the most soul-enriching activity in the world, it's true. Only a fool would deny this. But wait. Anon, we will see that the contrary is true.

The soul is sometimes fickle, fickle as can be. So we must humor the soul, go along to get along. Sometimes if you want to nourish your soul you must engage in an activity that is, on the surface of it, not fun. Like cleaning house. The startling thing about this is that when you finish cleaning it will be as if you gave your soul a mega-injection of spiritual Vitamin B complex. You will have a soul so nourished it will be as if you gave it spiritual steroids in massive quantities.

So screw up your courage and get out the cleaning gear. Where would you like to start? Maybe you know darn good and well where you should start, the basement, maybe, or the garage. Shudder. Don't start there, as there is no sense in getting carried away too soon. Start out slowly and work up.

The first thing to do is put on some music you enjoy. If you're alone, put on music no one likes except you. Crank it up loud, but if you live in an apartment building not *too* loud. If you're not sure what kind of music best suits cleaning house, consider Ragtime music. It fits, you know. *Rag* time, get it? Highly recommended is *The Complete Works of Scott Joplin*, available on CD and audio cassettes on the LaserLight label. Lively, foot-tapping music!

Go after the bathroom(s). Scrub those toilets. Be kind. Dear little johns, what would we do without them? Clean those sinks so they sparkle! Polish those mirrors! Do a major number on the tub and/or shower. Whoa. Now you're cookin'.

Dust, dust, dust. Vacuum, vacuum, vacuum. Polish, polish, polish. Mop the kitchen floor and give it a heavy coat of wax. You are going to love cooking in this kitchen now. Get after those Venetian blinds; dust each one of those little devils. If it's been a long time, take each set down, hang it up outside, go after it with a rag and soapy water, then hose it down and let it dry. If the weather is not warm and sunny, do not do this.

Finally, clean the basement or garage, whichever is the part of your place you want to clean the least. Just get in there and *do* it. Get it done, get it over with; you are going to feel so good when this is over.

Okay. House or apartment all clean? Open a cool drink, sit down, put your feet up, and drink that drink. Then go soak in that nice clean tub. (See suggestion #94.)

99 ◆ *Sleep*

O NE OF THE MOST important ways to nourish your soul in the entire soul-nourishing repertoire is to sleep. Catch z's. Sack out. Press sheets. Hit the hay. Most people today don't sleep nearly enough, so resolve to sleep more. If you use many of the other suggestions in this book, you will find it easy to sleep more because your soul will be tuned in to the nourishment sleep can bring.

Gilbert Keith Chesterton, one of the most quotable English-speaking persons of the entire twentieth century, once remarked that sleeping is one of the most perfect activities known to the human race. Chesterton himself enjoyed sleeping and lying in bed a great deal. He said that lying in bed only lacked a pencil long enough to doodle on the ceiling with. Truer words were never spoken.

To sleep is to turn loose of it all. To sleep is to give up control over your life and yourself. To sleep is a kind of prayer in itself, a prayer that says to the Divine Mystery, "I did all I could, now you take over." It takes a lot of faith to sleep and sleep well. It takes a lot of faith to abandon yourself to the restful unconsciousness the soul needs so much.

A wry wit, at the end of the day, was in the habit of commenting to whoever was listening, "Time to head home to the arms of Morpheus." Falling on certain ears this remark caused concern and, yes, some scandal. My word. The man is living in sin. Or the man is a drug addict. Odds bodkins.

No need to worry. This was simply the witty one's way of saying that he was bound for home where he would get some much needed sleep. Morpheus, you see, was — still is, for that matter — the god of dreams in the *Metamorphoses* of the first-century Roman poet Ovid.

Sleep is one of the most healing of human activities, and you should do more of it. Give it a go; you and your soul will be glad you did. Whenever you get the chance, take a cat nap. Doze. It will do your soul good.

100 ◆ *Take a Vacation You Can't Afford*

S AY, this is a good one. The idea is not to be fiscally irresponsible; the idea is to admit that you need a vacation at least one week long at least once a year. At the very least. Mere lack of funds ready to hand should not stop you.

The 1960s Irish radical Bernadette Devlin wrote an autobiography called *The Price of My Soul*. In this memoir she told of growing up with parents who had their souls in the right place. If Bernadette and her siblings heard their parents saying, "There'll be days when we'll be dead," they knew they were about to take a vacation they couldn't afford.

Indeed, there will be days when you'll be dead. So live now. Don't be completely irresponsible; just be willing to stick your neck out a little and take a bit of a financial risk. The idea is not to max out every credit card in the house. The idea is, if it's summer and you don't have the money to pay for the usual modest family vacation, but the finances are in reasonably good shape and you don't foresee being out of work in the next six months, then go ahead. Borrow the money for the vacation. Or run the credit card up a few hundred bucks. Or whatever.

Family life, in particular, is about collecting memories, so go out and collect some. Not to say they will all be *pleasant* memories; we all know more about family life than that. But they will be memories.

Do not, repeat, do not go into debt way beyond the dictates of reason in order to take the little tykes to Disneyland. Places like this, Disneyland in particular, are way overhyped. If you have never been there before, you will be disappointed. So don't bother. It's nice, it's clean. But it's not worth going into debt beyond reason, and the lines you have to stand in during the summer months are killers.

Take a vacation you can't afford, but keep it nice and simple and keep the debt within reason. You know what "within reason" means for you. Don't deny that you do. A vacation nourishes the soul, so take one.

101 ◆ *Overcome Dichotomies*

LOOK IT UP. Here is what it says: "Dichotomy: Division into two usually contradictory parts." It's what this book is about, overcoming the usual, but false, dichotomy between soul and body. We are our body, and we are our soul, and the two should not be divided. Do unto yourself as you would have others do unto you. Take care of yourself spiritually (bodily) and you will take care of yourself bodily (spiritually).

Nourish your ordinary ol' bod and your soul will thank you for it. Give your soul the time and attention it deserves, and your bod will benefit. It's as simple as that.

Now, this book deserves a good ending, an ending that says in a nutshell and metaphorically, if not analogically, everything the author has tried to say in so many trying ways. So here it is, a true story about Groucho and Harpo Marx and about overcoming dichotomies. It also has Zen koan-like qualities, so don't think about it; just let the story settle into your consciousness where, one day, it may startle you into some kind of enlightenment.

Here is the true story:

Groucho and Harpo were invited to a snobsville bachelor dinner prior to a Very Expensive Wedding. The two brothers noticed that the automatic elevator opened directly into the dining rooms of the various floors of the building where the dinner was held. As the elevator went up Groucho and Harpo arranged a surprise for the group of men at the dinner. They walked out of the elevator carrying their clothes in valises wearing nothing but top hats.

To the chagrin of Groucho and Harpo, their action evoked not raucous roars of male laughter but a great many female shrieks. The bride was entertaining her friends on the floor above the bachelor dinner, and Groucho and Harpo had pressed the wrong button.

Hey, they had the right idea.

Also by Mitch Finley...

Heavenly Helpers: St. Anthony and St. Jude
Amazing True Stories of Answered Prayers

True stories of prayers made to two of the most popular saints: Jude and Anthony. The results include physical healings, spiritual healings, lost things found, hopeless situations that come to a good end, and much more.

0-8245-1435-1 $16.95 hc

Whispers of Love
Encounters with Deceased Relatives and Friends

More and more Americans are experiencing the actual presence of loved ones after their deaths. Here are seventy-five comforting true stories.

0-8245-1491-2 $19.95 hc

Everybody Has a Guardian Angel

"A positive, gently humorous treatment of Finley's own years in Catholic schools....Nuggets of wisdom that cross denominational barriers are sprinkled throughout." — *Library Journal*

0-8245-1343-2 $10.95 pbk

The Joy of Being Catholic

"Mitch Finley has found in Catholicism exquisite, exhilarating, rambunctious, and even infectious joy. So read *The Joy of Being Catholic* — with joy!"
— Patrick F. McManus, author of *How I Got This Way*

0-8245-1551-X $16.95 hc

At your book store, or from the Crossroad Publishing Company, 370 Lexington Avenue, New York, NY 10017 (please add $3.00 for the first book, $1.00 for each additional book, for postage and handling fees). Please write us also for a free catalog of Crossroad books.

Thank you for reading
101 Ways to Nourish Your Soul.